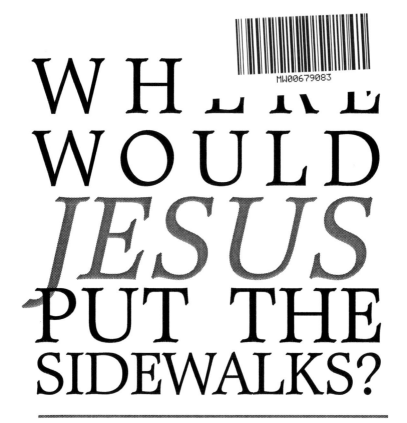

WHERE WOULD *JESUS* PUT THE SIDEWALKS?

A STUDY OF FAITH & POLITICS: A MOST HOLY ALLIANCE

by

DR. JAMES A. NELSON

INKWATER PRESS

Please note: All biblical references, unless otherwise noted, are from the New Revised Standard Version Bible, copyright 1989 by the Division of Christian Education of the National Council of the Churches of Christ in the U.S.A.

Cover and interior designed by Masha Shubin

www.inkwaterpress.com

ISBN 1-59299-083-5

Publisher: Inkwater Press

Printed in the U.S.A.

TABLE OF CONTENTS

ACKNOWLEDGEMENTS VII

INTRODUCTION IX

BE NOT AFRAID! 1

The Right To Speak 1

Our Obligation as Christians 4

Beware the Dangers 6

Turn the Other Cheek 7

Actions Speak Louder than Words 8

Going Too Far 11

Need for Balance 12

PURGE THE EVIL FROM YOUR MIDST – CAPITAL PUNISHMENT 18

The Facts 18

What the Bible Says 19

Arguments Against 23

Arguments For 26

Crimes of Passion v. Crimes of Logic 27

The Means Must Justify the Ends 28

Spiritual Death 30

MORALITY IS IN THE EYE OF THE BEHOLDER .. 38

What is Morality? 38

Strict Father Morality 40

Nurturant Parent Morality 44

Current Issues from a Moral Perspective 47
Conclusion 51

TURN THE OTHER CHEEK? – JUSTIFIED USES OF VIOLENCE 56
Is Violence Ever Justified? 56
Pacifism 57
Just War 61
Just Intention 64
Just Proportionality 65
Holy War 66
A Word About Forgiveness 69

THE BREATH OF LIFE – ABORTION & EUTHANASIA 74
Questions 75
The Beginning 76
In the Middle 80
The End 85
The Essence of Life 88

TEACHING THE CHILDREN & SCHOOL PRAYER 92
Tell Your Children 92
School Prayer 95
Who is Responsible? 98
What Do We Teach? 100
Public Education 101

APPENDIX A 107

APPENDIX B: SECOND TUESDAYS 109

APPENDIX C-1: CONTRARY TO CONVENTIONAL WISDOM 112

APPENDIX C-2: COMPARTMENTALIZING OUR FAITH 115

APPENDIX C-3: IN PRAISE OF EXTREMISTS 118

APPENDIX C-4: DEATH VS. COMPASSION 121

APPENDIX C-5: SOMETHING TO DIE FOR 124

APPENDIX C-6: STATE-SPONSORED PRAYER ERODES RELIGIOUS FREEDOM 127

APPENDIX C-7: KEEP GOVERNMENT OUT OF RELIGION 130

APPENDIX C-8: FUNDING FAITH-BASED AFTER-SCHOOL PROGRAMS 133

BIBLIOGRAPHY 136

ACKNOWLEDGEMENTS

First and foremost I thank God for all the help God has given me with the writing of this book: for the guidance, the direction, and the words. I would also like to thank the Rev. Dr. John Page, Jr., pastor of the Sandy Springs United Methodist Church in Atlanta, Georgia, for his guidance and input as my Project Director for my Doctor of Ministry Degree; and the members of the Sandy Springs Congregation who participated in what I hope will be the first of many discussion groups based on this book.

I thank Bishop B. Michael Watson, and the South Georgia Annual Conference of the United Methodist Church for giving me the time off I need to complete the work on this project and to finish my Doctor of Ministry Degree. The majority of the work for this book I did as part of that degree from The Graduate Theological Foundation in Donaldson, Indiana. I also need to express my appreciation to the *Wesleyan Christian Advocate*, and the *Georgia Guardian* which have printed my articles on "Faith and Politics" since 1995.

Last, but certainly not least, I thank my wife, Marty. She has been my muse throughout my years in ministry, and in particular for this project. I greatly appreciate her support, her editing, her input, her patience, and especially her love. I could not have completed this work without all the sacrifices she has made.

INTRODUCTION

The Church is irrelevant. It has become, especially in the last half of the twentieth century, disestablished. That is a rather painful and heart-wrenching statement to make, but the truth is that whereas the Church and its members were once persecuted for their beliefs, today they suffer a worse fate: they are ignored. Admittedly, there are a number of people for whom the church is extremely relevant, but unfortunately, that number is continually decreasing. In recent years, fewer and fewer people are members of or even associated with a church.

Whereas once churches were the center of many communities and places where the majority of people went to discuss the issues of the day that were important to their lives, today the majority of churches sit empty most of time and the important issues of the day are usually avoided. And, whereas once members of the clergy were treated with respect, today they and their opinions are largely ignored.

Unfortunately, the reason the Church has become irrelevant is that too many local churches choose to only be concerned with and preach about irrelevant issues. These churches are not addressing the important issues people face in their daily lives, which are the very issues people want addressed. After September 11, 2001, many previously unchurched individuals sought refuge and spiritual guidance in churches. Unfortunately, too many churches did not know how to respond, or responded with platitudes. Within two months, most of those individuals had left again. People are less interested in a cute story about a young shepherd boy who slays a giant with his slingshot, than they are in how to slay the giants in their own lives: an alcoholic and/or abusive father; a mother with Alzheimer's; a pregnant, unwed teenage daughter; a son on drugs; a wife and mother sent to fight a war in a distant land; depression; job insecurity; a retirement account wiped out by unscrupulous business practices; violence in schools; sexism, racism, classism; glass ceilings for women and minorities; etc. People want to know how to put food on their table and a roof over their head, not miracle stories about feeding 5,000 other people. People want the church to answer the question, "How can faith make my life better? How does going to church keep the wolves away from the door? How is a 2000 year old book, the Bible, relevant for my life today?"

The Church needs to address these issues from a theological perspective, hold discussions about them, and help people figure out how to respond to these issues as good Christians in the twenty-first century. The Church needs to help people live lives of faith. If people believe they are doing all right without faith and without attending church, then the church has failed. If people do see the difference that practicing their faith can have in their lives, they can easily find a better way to spend Sunday mornings.

In other words, if it ever hopes to reestablish itself, the Church must once again become relevant in people's lives.

That does not mean we should abandon the scriptures and the stories of our faith traditions. First and foremost churches need to be the places where the Good News that Jesus Christ is Lord and the ruler of our lives is proclaim. After all, what would a Christian Church be without Christ? Churches need to be places where people encounter the living God, and make the God connection. They need to be places where people can grow in their faith and spend time in prayer; places where they are encouraged to live the life Jesus calls them to lead.

As Christians we cannot be ashamed of our faith. We need to proudly proclaim that we are Christians even if we are embarrassed by others who misuse the faith for their own purposes. Just because some people use the Bible and Christianity as a weapon and as a means of creating hatred and divisiveness in the world, does not mean we should deny being Christians. We do not need to apologize for what we know to be the Truth; an error often made by those who are considered to be theologically liberal. When we do, we allow others to define what it means to be a Christian, which is often far from the Truth. Nevertheless, it is up to us to set the proper example of love, compassion, and forgiveness for the rest of the world. Besides, Jesus tells us, "but whoever denies me before others, I also will deny before my Father in heaven." (Matthew 10:33).

Admittedly it is a gross generalization, but liberal theologians tend to put too much emphasis on doing and not enough on proclaiming. Conservatives on the other hand often appear, as the old saying goes, "so heavenly minded, they are no earthly good." They spend more time talking about the faith, than they spend living it. Both extremes miss the point that what we need is a blend of proclamation and action.

Christians need to reach out in love and compassion to others, to help them, and tell them about Jesus. But, as Jesus says, "If you do good to those who do good to you, what credit is that to you?" (Luke 6:33a). Therefore, we need to be especially helpful to those who cannot or will not repay us. To be effective at helping, we need the love of God within us and to let our light shine forth for all the world to see. If others do not see Christ when they look at those of us who claim to be Christians, why would they ever want to become one?

Relevance also requires that the Church be involved in the political process, but in a way that does not establish or even call for a national religion. The Church needs to be a prophetic voice crying out in the wilderness; it needs to be the conscience of the nation, which holds our leaders and ourselves accountable to the principles set forth by Jesus. However, those of us living in the United States must be particularly careful to avoid the temptation of becoming a totalitarian state like a few Islamic nations, which put religious correctness ahead of individual rights and freedoms. Nevertheless, Christians need to come out of the pews, and be more active in the communities in which they live and in the world at large. It is incumbent upon all Christians to be aware of the world around them, of what is going on, and how it affects their beliefs.

For example, even if and where communities install sidewalks can have theological implications: since walking makes us healthier, we take care of the temple God has given us when we use sidewalks; walking helps us reduce fossil fuel emissions resulting in less pollution, which makes us better stewards of the world God entrusted to us; and walking reduces our dependence on foreign oil, making us more self-sufficient and easier for us to make the right decision when faced with moral dilemmas. So, do we put sidewalks in poor neighborhoods first where the people who cannot afford cars need the safety sidewalks provide, or in wealthier neighborhoods where only those few who want a little exercise would use them? After all, "as you do for the least of these" is a theological principle. In God's eyes, what we do about sidewalks may be as important to our salvation as what we do about war and violence.

How we vote on Election Day says more about what we believe than what we profess on Sunday morning. It is where we put our faith into action. What we truly believe becomes apparent based on the people and positions we support and vote for. Most of the Hebrew Scriptures are about kings and advisors to kings, the prophets who encouraged the kings and the people to obey the commandments of God. In the New Testament, Jesus calls on us to reject what the forces of this world often see as important: self-gratification, power, wealth, etc.; and to focus on what God wants: taking care of one another, and acknowledging God's presence in our lives and in the world. Churches and their leaders must become the prophets of today pointing out our inconsistencies, holding us accountable for our actions, and calling us to be like Jesus who was always in-the-face of secular society. For example, we cannot say we believe in welcoming strangers, yet wish to put a wall around the nation; thereby, keeping immigrants out, nor can we deny those who are here legally the benefits the rest of us enjoy. We cannot say we believe in supporting the widows and orphans (especially those who are born poor) yet support ending welfare payments and aid to dependent children for needy families. Nor, can we say we believe in forgiveness and loving our neighbors, yet at the same time support a war in which we drop bombs on innocent non-combatants who are already suffering from the harsh regimes we claim to be trying to eliminate.

The Church should constantly be challenging the political forces of this world to do a better job taking care of God's creation. The Book of Genesis tells us that we have dominion over the earth and all that is in it, which means we are responsible for it. If it gets polluted, it is our fault for not exercising proper dominion. We have the treasures of the world to use, but not to abuse. We need to use what God has given us for good, for the betterment of all of God's children, but not for our own enrichment at the expense of future generations. That does not mean we have to sacrifice development and human needs to save endangered species, but neither can we just indiscriminately destroy and pollute the environment because it is easier and/or less costly than being good stewards.

The Church should demand governments take care of the poor and the outcast of society. Jesus came to lift up the lowly and bring down the high and mighty. The Church needs to confront governments when they are wrong and tilted toward the powerful, which by the way refers to nearly all governments, and demand they protect the rights of those who cannot protect themselves. After all, Jesus did call on us to feed the hungry, clothe the naked, and care for the sick and infirmed.

There is one caveat, however. History tells us that political involvement by the Church can be a double-edged sword. The Church must be careful and not allow itself to be co-opted by the government. It cannot allow an opportunity for power, for status and position to interfere with its doing what is right. Historically, religious people have allowed governments to control them in exchange for the Church's right to exist. Once Constantine had his vision and made Christianity an officially recognized religion, the Church began to be more conciliatory toward and less critical of the government. Charlemagne used the Church when he insisted the Pope crown him

Emperor, so he would have the status of being God's chosen ruler of the Holy Roman Empire. New Protestant denominations succeeded in gaining power during the Reformation because the governments where they were located supported them against the Roman Pope. Kings and princes throughout Europe had grown weary of being told what to do by an Italian, so they helped theological reformers establish new denominations, which would be beholden and loyal to them: Luther in Germany, Zwingli in Zurich, and Calvin in Geneva. In England, Henry VIII formed his own church in part because the Roman Pope refused to sanction Henry's divorce from his first wife. When the Portuguese challenged the Church over land in South America, the Church acquiesced because it feared losing power and being expelled from Portugal and its territories. For years the Russian Orthodox Church was tightly aligned with the Czarist regimes, which led to its downfall when the Communists seized power in 1917. Today, the Roman Catholic Church is losing power and status in South America as the regimes it once supported are being overthrown by more democratic governments. It is dangerous for the church to sell out for power and status to any government, corrupt or not, because often when that government is toppled, so is the church.

Churches should influence the government, not the other way around. The freedom of religion guaranteed by the Constitution of the United States does not guarantee freedom "from" religion. The Bible has several examples, particularly in the Hebrew

Scriptures, where those of faith were to guide those with political power. When Saul failed to wait for Samuel, and took it upon himself to offer up a sacrifice to God, Samuel chastised him because even though Saul was the King, he was still required to keep the commandments of God (1 Samuel 13).

If we would read the Bible as a theological text, instead of as a definitive historical document, we would find a lot more direction on subjects not addressed in those texts. The Bible has no concept of bio-ethics, gene manipulation, in vitro fertilization, sterilization, over population, etc. It has mixed messages about abortion, homosexuality, and other controversial issues when read too narrowly, and too literally. Reading the Bible, as well as other ancient scriptures, as theological texts enlightening us about our relationship to God and teaching us how to respect one another, gives us the insight we need to make decisions in today's complex world. Besides, we need to remember God is not dead. God is still talking to us, and communicating with us. If we say God told us everything 2000 years ago and that is all we need, then God may as well be dead if He is no longer active or needed in the world.

The purpose of this book is to encourage discussions on some of the topics relevant to our lives today. It is my hope that reading this book will generate more questions than answers. Churches need to set up classes and small group discussions around controversial issues based on biblical and traditional religious arguments. The six chapters in this study are not intended to be inclusive and should be just the beginning. I hope that after discussing these issues, you will be inspired to look at others, which are relevant in the lives of the members of your individual congregations. And, I hope preachers will begin, or continue as the case may be, preaching politics from the pulpit. We need to go back to the concept of preaching with the Bible in one hand and a newspaper in the other if we ever hope to reestablish the church in modern society.

I am not advocating that churches all over the nation begin programs aimed at curing the ills of society. Churches do not need to become social program generators. There are a multitude of programs that already exist in every community with which members of congregations can get involved. Churches themselves need to be places of worship, which nurture, empower, and support people to go out into the world and to do the work and the will of God. They need to be places where people can hear the call of God for their lives, and where they can return to celebrate all that God has helped them to accomplish. The traditional church still has relevance as the place in the world where people can gather to worship and praise the Lord their God as a community of believers who love and care for one another.

God is calling on us in the Church to move beyond where we are, to move to new heights unforeseeable just a few short years ago. We do not need fancy buildings, which are little more than monuments to our own glory, in order to worship God. We just need hearts that are pure, that long to live at peace with others, and that are open to and accepting of all God's children.

At the end of the book, you will find several Appendixes. The first, Appendix A, is a suggested outline for a discussion group based on the six readings. Appendix B outlines another program a church could implement to address these and other issues of importance to society. And, Appendix C contains eight reprints out of the hundreds of articles I have written since 1994 on the subject of "Faith and Politics" for newspapers and magazines. Although I have been writing columns since 1994, I have been interested in this subject my entire life.

May God guide us all, as we begin this journey together.

WHERE WOULD JESUS PUT THE SIDEWALKS?

BE NOT AFRAID!

Suggested Scripture reading: Lev 5:1,5-6; 1Sam 14:1-23; Ezek 33:1-9; Mt 18:15-20; Rev. 21:8.

The Right To Speak

Christianity is a communal religion. It has continued to exist because communities of believers have come together to worship. There are many ministries, which can only be performed, or at least be more efficiently performed, by communities. However, every community is made up of individuals, and there are some ministries, which can only be effectively performed by individuals. As individual Christians we have the responsibility to keep the faith alive, and to act in certain ways. Some of those required actions might be quite dangerous, but as Jesus tells us, "[24]... 'If any want to become my followers, let them deny themselves and take up their cross and follow me. [25]For those who want to save their life will lose it, and those who lose their life for my sake will find it.'" (Matthew 16:24b-25)

The First Amendment to the U.S. Constitution says, "Congress shall make no laws respecting an establishment of religion, or prohibiting the free exercise thereof; or abridging the freedom of speech, or of the press; or the right of the people peaceable to assemble, and to petition the Government for a redress of grievances."[1] In other words, we Americans have the right to worship as we choose, speak our minds when we feel like it, gather together for whatever purpose we feel appropriate, and to seek restitution from the Government. We can criticize governments at all levels, as well as the representatives thereof without fear of recrimination. We can even criticize the President in time of war if we choose; and although unpopular, we can burn the American Flag just to make a point. We do not have to go along with the majority at any time or in respect to any matter. In fact, unity of thought is un-American.

Differences of opinion are what make America great, and help keep us free. Those who call for everyone to agree, to go along with the government are the real threat to the American way of life. We will not get the best we can have if the opposition is afraid to speak out because they are afraid of being called un-American. My greatest fear in times of national tragedy is that our freedom will not be something that is taken from us, but something we will graciously, yet foolishly, give away.

The question then becomes, do we as Christians, in light of the teachings found in the Bible, have not only the right but the obligation to speak out when we see government, or individuals acting in ways contrary to the will of God? In Leviticus we read,

> [1]When any of you sin in that you have heard a public adjuration to testify and – though

> able to testify as one who has seen or learned of the matter – does not speak up, you are subject to punishment.... [5]When you realize your guilt in any of these, you shall confess the sin that you have committed. [6]And you shall bring to the LORD, as your penalty for the sin that you have committed, a female from the flock, a sheep or a goat, as a sin offering; and the priest shall make atonement on your behalf for your sin. (Leviticus 5:1,5-6).

God seems to be telling us that we cannot remain silent when we have knowledge of a sin having been committed. If we extend that idea, it becomes clear we also cannot remain silent when we believe the government, or representatives of the government are doing wrong. We have to obligation to speak out.

God does not like cowards. At the end of *The Book of Revelation*, we read that the one seated on the throne in John's vision said, "But as for the cowardly, the faithless, the polluted, the murderers, the fornicators, the sorcerers, the idolaters, and all liars, their place will be in the lake that burns with fire and sulfur, which is the second death." (Revelation 21:8). The first trait mentioned in that long list is the "cowardly." How many times in scripture when God, or a messenger of God (an angel) appears do they begin with the words, "Do not be afraid"? God wants and expects us to have courage, and to always do the right thing. We must show God we can be trusted. To act cowardly is to lack faith, to not trust in the Lord our God. Faith, true faith, gives us courage. We must use that courage in the face of whatever trials may come our way in life. We must be willing to stand up and be heard even when our position is unpopular. We must not be afraid.

Our Obligation as Christians

When we see the government moving in a direction, which begins to erode the rights of its citizens; we are obligated to speak out. There is a familiar quote attributed to Martin Niemoeller in the aftermath of World War II which goes,

> In Germany they came first for the Communists, and I didn't speak up because I wasn't a Communist. Then they came for the Jews, and I didn't speak up because I wasn't a Jew. Then they came for the trade unionists, and I didn't speak up because I wasn't a trade unionist. Then they came for the Catholics, and I didn't speak up because I was a Protestant. Then they came for me, and by that time no one was left to speak up.[2]

We cannot wait until a policy directly affects us before we begin to object. We live in the United States, and as such, we not only have the right and the opportunity to object, we have the obligation. If we do not object when someone else is affected, we may not have the right in the future to object when we are personally affected.

The history of Christianity is replete with stories of martyrs who gave up their lives, often in brutal ways, but who had the courage to remain true to their beliefs. Even the twentieth century had numerous examples of people who refused to do the popular or politically expedient thing, but who instead chose to do the right thing regardless of the consequences. Take for example, Dietrich Bonhoeffer who was safe in the United States in 1939, yet chose to return to his home in Nazi-Germany to minister to his people. His anti-Nazi sentiments, statements, and actions eventually led to his arrest. He was imprisoned, and ultimately hanged at the age of 39 just days before the war ended. Bonhoeffer understood the need for action. Among his *Letters and Papers from Prison* is a brief article he called, "Stations on the Road to Freedom," those stations are discipline, action, suffering, and death. Regarding "Action" he wrote,

To do and dare – not what you would, but what is right. Never to hesitate over what is within your power, but boldly to grasp what lies before you. Not in the flight of fancy, but only in the deed there is freedom. Away with timidity and reluctance! Out into the storm of event, sustained only by the commandment of God and your faith, and freedom will receive your spirit with exultation.[3]

Only by boldly acting out our faith can we truly experience freedom.

Beware the Dangers

If we are not careful, the real tragedy of September 11, 2001 could easily become not so much what the terrorists did on that day, but what we do to ourselves in the aftermath. We run the risk of sacrificing our rights, and our freedom for the illusion of security. But as Martin Niemoeller is reminding us in the above quote, the reduction of rights is a slippery slope. At first it affects only those on the outer edges of society, those who do not belong to the dominant culture. But once the erosion begins, it will eventually lead to a loss of freedom for everyone. We must have the courage to stand up against proposed reductions in our freedoms.

There are those who believe you must go along to get along. And, in some ways they are right. If you go along and do whatever those in authority tell you to, you have a better chance of surviving to a ripe old age. The problem with that philosophy is that it is selfish. It is based on the concept of watching out for yourself, and not caring about the suffering of others. On the other hand, if you speak out, you run the risk of being arrested and possibly even executed as Bonhoeffer was. When we follow the biblical message to put the welfare of others ahead of our own, we risk being seen as subversive. Standing up for the underdog, for those who are left out of society is not easy, and takes courage; however, the means we use to respond is equally as important.

Turn the Other Cheek

In the Sermon on the Mount, Jesus tells us, "If anyone strikes you on the right cheek, turn the other also." (Matthew 5:39b). How are we to interpret that commandment in light of the events of September 11? Do we just do nothing? Do we allow ourselves to be further victimized by terrorists who are intent on creating a new world order: one, which does not include us? Of course not. We do need to turn the other cheek, but as Jesus did in a defiant manner. He is not telling us to lay down and be a door mat for anyone and everyone who wants to attack us, but to stand up to them and defiantly turn the other cheek; in other words, to not be afraid. We need to say to those who committed these terrorist acts to go ahead and try again, but we will not cower in fear. Jesus is telling us not to change who we are, what we believe in, or what we hold most dear just because someone has hurt us or threatens to hurt us. We must go on. And, even more importantly he was reminding us not to repay evil for evil; that we cannot be true to the Hebrew Scripture imperative to remove the evil from among us by becoming evil ourselves. Jesus understood that by resorting to the tactics of those who are evil, we become evil and create even more evil in the world. At the same time, we cannot lie down in the face of evil and allow it to continue to harm innocent people.

We need to read this passage from the Sermon on the Mount in conjunction with Jesus' statement in Chapter 10, "Do not fear those who kill the body but cannot kill the soul; rather fear him who can destroy both soul and body in hell." (Matthew 10:28). Responding to evil with evil destroys both soul and body, and "they" win. When we respond to evil by allowing the government to erode the rights of others, particularly those on the fringes of society, we have allowed them to destroy both soul and body. We cannot allow ourselves to become as oppressive as those who wish to destroy us. We win; we do the will of God when we are not afraid, when we turn the other cheek, and when we go about the business of fully living our lives.

Actions Speak Louder than Words

As a nation we may need to do something more than simply turn the other cheek when it comes to terrorism; but as individuals, especially Christians, turning the other cheek is exactly what we need to do. We need to stand-up, defiantly, and say to those who are trying to end our way of life that we will not let them. We will not hide. We will not cower in fear. We will continue to do what we have always done.

Stories about people who acted without fear can be found throughout the Bible. In 1 Samuel, for example, we have the stories of Jonathon and David and the courage they showed, which led to great victories for the Israelites. Jonathan was the son of Saul, the King of Israel. Saul and the Israelites were encamped on one hill, and the Philistines on another. Saul was consulting the priests that were with him, and waiting for an omen from God. He was afraid to act on his own. Jonathan, on the other hand, knew that something had to be done, so

> 6Jonathan said to the young man who carried his armor, "Come, let us go over to the garrison of these uncircumcised; it may be that the LORD will act for us; for nothing can hinder the LORD from saving by many or by few." 7His armor-bearer said to him, "Do all that your mind inclines to. I am with you; as your mind is, so is mine." 8Then Jonathan said, "Now we will cross over to those men and will show ourselves to them. 9If they say to us, 'Wait until we come to you,' then we will stand still in our place, and we will not go up to them. 10But if they say, "come up to us,' then we will go up; for the LORD has given them into our hand. That will be the sign for us." 11So both of them showed themselves to the garrison of the Philistines; and the Philistines said, "Look, Hebrews are coming out of the holes where they have hidden themselves." 12The men of the garrison hailed Jonathan and his armor-bearer, saying, "Come up to us, and we will show you something." Jonathan said to his armor-bearer, "Come up after me; for the LORD has given them into the hand of Israel." 13Then Jonathan climbed up on his hands and feet, with his armor-bearer fol-

> lowing after him. The Philistines fell before Jonathan, and his armor-bearer, coming after him, killed them. [14]In that first slaughter Jonathan and his armor-bearer killed about twenty men within an area about half a furrow long in an acre of land. [15]There was a panic in the camp, in the field, and among all the people; the garrison and even the raiders trembled; the earth quaked; and it became a very great panic. (1 Samuel 14:6-15).

Jonathan and his armor-bearer won the day. The Philistines were routed, and the Israelites, inspired by Jonathan's courage, pursued and defeated them. Had Jonathan waited for Saul to get around to doing something, it could easily have been too late. He did not "know" God would be with him, but he knew he had to trust that God would. Jonathan understood God can work through us and with us, but God will not do all the work for us. Jonathan did not even know if he was right; he just knew somebody had to do something. At times we must be willing to grab the proverbial bull by the horns and act. Courage is an integral part of being a good Christian.

Later in the Book of Samuel we read about Goliath taunting the Israelites causing them to cower in fear. No one would go out to meet him. David, however, still a young man, decided no one should be able to insult the God of Israel and live. Therefore, he agreed to go out and face the giant, Goliath himself. David wore no armor, and took with him only his slingshot and five smooth stones. Goliath laughed at the sight of a boy coming out as the champion of the Israelites, as the Philistines had laughed when Jonathan and his armor-bearer came against them. When Goliath moved toward David, probably still laughing; David ran toward him, put a stone in his sling, slung it at Goliath, and "struck the Philistine on his forehead; the stone sank into his forehead, and he fell face down on the ground." (1 Samuel 17:49b). Again, this act of courage inspired the Israelites and with God's help led to the defeat of the Philistines. David, like Jonathan before him, trusted that God would be on his side.

Going Too Far

I once asked a class the question, "What would you do if you were a child of Abraham, your sacred places had been defiled by foreigners, those occupying your land were turning your fellow citizens away from God and from following God's commandments, and finally you found yourself in exile." The answers I got back were mainly about defying those now in positions of authority, and remaining true to your faith. They also talked about forming a resistance, and trying to regain power. They wanted to regain control of their own destiny.

I then asked, "What if you are a child of Abraham, your sacred places of Mecca and Medina are being defiled by foreigners from the West led by the United States, the commandments of God as contained in the Koran are not being adhered to, and you are in exile in Afghanistan?" Because, in essence the answers they were giving were consistent with acts of terrorism by Islamic fundamentalists. As has often been stated, one person's terrorist is another person's freedom fighter, or upholder of the faith. You can imagine the discussion that led to. People do not like to be compared to those with whom they disagree or do not like; yet that does not change the facts.

Selectively using scripture can be dangerous. By just quoting a few passages from the Bible we could easily justify similar acts as those perpetrated on September 11. Fortunately, most Christians read enough of the Words of Jesus to know that violence is not the answer. We cannot win people to the faith, or maintain their loyalty and conviction at the point of a gun. More people come to the faith because we treat them with fairness, honesty, and decency. Let us be honest, there have been those who have claimed to be Christians over the years who have been guilty of acting with as much disregard for the lives and welfare of others out of their devotion to God, as those who commit acts of terrorism claiming to be faithful to the Koran.

Need for Balance

We must find a way to speak out when we believe someone is wrong, without violating his or her rights. In Ezekiel, God tells us we should be like watchmen on the tower and sound the alarm when we see danger coming; but if the people do not heed the warning, then their blood is on their hands and we are free. Jesus told his disciples when he sent them out by two's that if they came to a town or a house where they and their message were not welcomed, they should knock the dust from their feet and go on. He did not tell them to continue arguing with the people. He did not tell them to force the people to change their ways. He said to make your pitch and move on.

It is just human nature to want freedom, to have control over our own destiny. But, it is also human nature to not want others to have the same rights. We do not want other people to be able to do what they want, when they want, and how they want. We want them to be like us. We think our way is the best way, and the right way. That in and of itself is not bad. We need to believe that what we are doing is right. But we cannot, nor should we ever force someone else to be like us. We need to feel comfortable telling others when we believe they are wrong, but at the same time allow them to have their own views. And, we need to be gracious to others who want to tell us when they believe we are wrong. As Jesus stated in the Golden Rule, "In everything do to others as you would have them do to you...." (Matthew 7:12a). If we could all learn to treat others the way we want them to treat us, to respect them the way we want them to respect us; the world would be a better place to live.

In March 2000, I wrote an article entitled "In Praise of Extremists" (see Appendix C-3) defending the right of those on the outer edges of religious and political thought to voice their opinion. We need to listen to both sides of the argument, and quite often it is the extremists who "bring important issues to the table, and keep them in the public debate."[4] The truth is often somewhere in between. The extremists keep the rest of us honest, and if we pay attention, will keep us from drifting too far to one side or the other. However, we do not need these people in control, or in positions of authority. We need to hear them, but we should never allow them to lead.

Courage is faith. We need to speak out when we hear God calling us in a certain direction. Like Jonathan and David we cannot be afraid of the consequences, of what others might say, or whether or not we are even doing the right thing. Often doing nothing is the only "wrong" thing in life. As Christians we are called to an active faith, and we cannot be afraid. We can only overcome evil by facing it, or as Henry David Thoreau wrote in his book, *A Week on the Concord and Merrimack Rivers,* "We do not avoid evil by fleeing before it, but by rising above or diving below its plane."[5]

We must also remember Jesus' admonition in the conclusion to the Sermon on the Mount that words alone are not enough; they must be followed up by actions. For he says, "Not everyone who says to me, 'Lord, Lord,' will enter the kingdom of heaven, but only the one who does the will of my Father in Heaven." (Matthew 7:21). We must "do" the will of God and not just talk about it; for Jesus tell us that at the end of time he will declare to those who only talk about their faith but do not live it, "I never knew you; go away from me, you evil doers." (Matthew 7:23b).

Questions for Discussion

1. Should the Church speak out and/or take a stand on political issues, particularly if they have a moral element to them?

2. If so, what can the Church do without losing its tax-free status?

3. Should the Church worry about its tax status if the issue is one of deep moral conviction?

4. Can you stay a member of a congregation, whose theology and style of worship you agree with, if that church or local congregation takes a political stance you disagree with?

5. Can you support a candidate or a political party that takes a position that is contrary to your religious beliefs and/or moral principles?

6. What if you only disagree on a minor issue? What if it is a major issue, but still only one?

7. What, if any, issues are there today on which the church should take a stand and get involved with regarding (a) the world, (b) our nation, (c) our state or region, (d) our community, (e) our church?

8. Are your political views consistent with your religious beliefs? If not, what would you have to change to make them consistent?

Notes

[1]*Constitution of the United States,* Amendment I (1791)

[2] Martin Niemoeller, as cited in *Bartlett's Familiar Quotations*, Ed. John Bartlett & Justin Kaplan (Boston: Little, Brown and Company, 1992) 684.

[3] Dietrich Bonhoeffer, *Letter and Papers from Prison* (New York: The Macmillan Company, 1953) 228.

[4] Jim Nelson, "In Praise of Extremists," *The Wesleyan Christian Advocate* (March 17, 2000) 14.

[5] Henry David Thoreau, "A Week on the Concord and Merrimack Rivers," in *Walden and Other Writings by Henry David Thoreau*, Ed. Joseph Wood Krutch (New York: Bantam Books, 1962) 81.

PURGE THE EVIL FROM YOUR MIDST – CAPITAL PUNISHMENT

Suggested Scripture readings: Ex 20:13; Num 15:32-36; Deut 13:6-11; Deut 21:18-21 read in light of Lk 15:11-32; Jn 8:2-11.

The Facts

According to Amnesty International in the year 2000 China executed about 1000 individuals out of a population of over 1,000,000,000, or about one execution for every one million people. In that same year, Cuba executed five. The United States executed 87. According to the Texas Department of Prisons' website, of those executed in the U.S. forty were from Texas which has a population of 20,000,000, or about one execution for every 500,000 residents. That means in the year 2000, Texas executed twice as many people per-capita as China.

Of the 40 executions in Texas, 19 were white, 16 black, and 5 Hispanic. Of the 455 people on death row in Texas, 152 are white, 192 black, 106 Hispanic, and 5 other. Those numbers are not consistent with their demographics. On the surface it would appear we are not fairly administering the death penalty, nor are we holding all life in the same regard.

Does the mere fact that the Death Penalty is not administered fairly justify abolishing it? Maybe, maybe not. The Bible tells us that when someone does something wrong, we must purge the evil from our midst; nevertheless, we should at the very least reform the system.

What the Bible Says

There are numerous passages in the Torah, which call for the execution, usually by stoning, of individuals who violate the laws of God. In the book of Deuteronomy, the justification most often given for the death penalty is, "So you shall purge the evil from your midst; and all Israel will hear, and be afraid." The early Israelites were a nomadic people, and the only way they had to separate criminals from their community was through death. There was also a belief that people would remain faithful to the laws if they feared being executed for violating them.

In the Kings James Version, the Ten Commandments in both Exodus and Deuteronomy include the commandment, "Thou shalt not kill." In the NRSV, a more modern translation, the same verses read, "Thou shall not murder," which is probably a much more accurate rendering. Obviously, killing was not a problem in the Torah, or most of the Hebrew Scriptures for that matter. Murder, on the other hand, which is the unjustified killing of another human being, was against the law.

Those who use the Bible to justify the death penalty should not take too much comfort in that fact. If we look at some of the crimes, which God demands restitution be paid with a life, we may find them somewhat disturbing to our modern sensibilities. For example, in Deuteronomy 21:18-21a the law says

> 18If someone has a stubborn and rebellious son who will not obey his father and mother, who does not heed them when they discipline him, 19then his father and his mother shall take hold of him and bring him out to the elders of his town at the gate of that place. 20They shall say to the elders of his town, "This son of ours is stubborn and rebellious. He will not obey us. He is a glutton and a drunkard." 21Then all the men of the town shall stone him to death.

Are we prepared to begin executing our children when they are disobedient, and/or when they use drugs and alcohol? That is what it would take to be true to the Bible's call for the death penalty.

Another example, in which all of us are probably guilty and deserving of death, can be found in Numbers 15:32-35,

> 32When the Israelites were in the wilderness, they found a man gathering sticks on the

> Sabbath day. [33]Those who found him gathering sticks brought him to Moses, Aaron, and to the whole congregation. [34]They put him in custody, because it was not clear what should be done to him. [35]Then the LORD said to Moses, "The man shall be put to death; all the congregation shall stone him outside the camp."

Perhaps this is just the type of sin Jesus had in mind when he said "Let anyone among you who is without sin be the first to throw a stone at her." (John 8:7b). How many of us can honestly say that we are totally without sin? Do we then have the right to condemn someone else? Remember that James tells us, "For whoever keeps the whole law but fails in one point has become accountable for all of it." (James 2:10). In other words, if we have failed to keep the Sabbath we are no less guilty in the eyes of God than someone who has committed murder.

In the story of Achan, found in Joshua 7, his entire family is executed with him. The belief was that evil is contagious and passed from one generation to the next. Therefore, every member of the family was equally as guilty as the person who actually committed the crime. Should we execute a criminal's entire family, so we can purge future evil from our midst as well?

In his book, *What You Can Change & What You Can't*, Dr. Martin E.P. Seligman cites a Danish study concerning the effects of nature versus nurture on behavior.

> If neither the natural nor the adopted father had ever been convicted of a crime, 10.5 percent of the sons turned out to be criminals. If the adopted father was a criminal, but the natural father was not, 11.5 percent of the sons were criminals, and insignificant difference....
>
> If the natural father (whom the child had not seen since he was, at the most, six month old) was a criminal, but the adopted father was not, 22 percent of the sons were criminals. Crime rate is doubled by having "criminal genes."[1]

Perhaps the ancient Israelites were on to something. If we execute children with their parents, we may eliminate future problems.

Fortunately, the Bible contradicts itself later on. In Jeremiah 31:29-30, we read, "[29]In those days they shall no longer say: 'The parents have eaten sour grapes, and the children's teeth are set on edge.' [30]But all shall die for their own sins; the teeth of everyone who eats sour grapes shall be set on edge." And again in Ezekiel 18:20a, "The person who sins shall die. A child shall not suffer for the iniquity of the parent, nor a parent suffer for the iniquity of a child...." We are each responsible for our own sins, and will pay the penalty individually if not in this life, at least in the life to come. The theology in the Bible was an evolving work until it was finally canonized in the Fourth Century. I often wonder if we were still listening, what would God be saying to us today about the death penalty?

Arguments Against

"All of the early Christians writers who discussed capital punishment were absolutely opposed to it. Christians were instructed to not execute a criminal, to not attend public executions and even to not lay a charge against a person if it might eventually result in their execution."[2] Many denominations today are still adamantly opposed to the death penalty, especially when implemented as a part of a retributive justice system.

At the U.S. Catholic Conference in 1999, the Most Rev. Joseph A. Fiorenza, President of the National Conference of Catholic Bishops, stated, "We oppose the death penalty not just for what it does to those guilty of heinous crimes, but for what it does to all of us: it offers the tragic illusion that we can defend life by taking life."[3] The taking of any life diminishes us all.

Another argument against the death penalty concerns the possibility of executing an innocent person. In January 2000, Illinois Governor George Ryan imposed a moratorium on executions. He is an advocate of the death penalty, but found the number of death penalty cases being overturned by DNA and other additional evidence disturbing. Unfortunately, those problems are not unique to Illinois. The entire system is plagued by unfairness, racism, classism, and depends more on where a person lives and who their victim was than it does on what they did.

In 1972 the U.S. Supreme Court in Furman v. Georgia found the individual states' death penalty statutes lacking standards, which allowed too much discretion for judges and juries. Consequently, the various states revised their statutes, and in 1976 the Supreme Court upheld the new Georgia death penalty statute in Gregg v. Georgia. Since then, over 600 executions have been carried out in the United States, and there are over 3,500 men, women, and children currently on death row. However, can we really say the death penalty is any less capricious in its application now than it was before 1972?

Sister Helen Prejean of *Dead Man Walking* fame has said, "The death penalty is a poor person's issue. Always remember that: after all the rhetoric that goes on in the legislative assemblies, in the end, when the deck is cast out, it is the poor who are selected to die in this country."[4] In fact, the primary difference between those who receive the death penalty and those who do not for a similar action is in the quality of legal representation. "In California, the state with the largest death row population (513), less than 2 percent were represented at trial by retained counsel."[5]

Most defendants in capital cases are represented by court-appointed lawyers. Quite often these lawyers are paid as little as $20 to $40 per hour. "Some states limit the amount of compensation a court-appointed attorney can receive in a death penalty case to as little as $2,000. (Compare this to the $14 million price tag on the first trial of Erik and Lyle Menendez which ended in a hung jury.)"[6] In fact, "Murderers who have the economic means to hire their own attorneys never, for all intents and purposes, receive a death sentence, no matter how terrible their crimes."[7] Without adequate representation, what chance do most defendants have?

Another problem is race. Not so much the race of the defendant as the race of the victim. Let's face it, non-whites are much more likely to receive a death sentence than whites. But even more insidious is the fact that in the United States as a whole about half of all people murdered are black, however 82% of executions have been for the murder of someone who was white. "Georgia prosecutors seek the death penalty in 70 percent of cases involving crimes committed by blacks against whites, but they seek the death penalty in less that 35 percent of cases involving other racial combinations."[8] Are white victims lives more valuable than the lives of other races?

The best evidence for the capriciousness of the administration of the death penalty in the United States can be found in the mere fact that whether a defendant is sentenced to death or not depends more on where they live than what they did. For example, Connecticut only has five inmates on death row, and Kansas two, while California has 513, and Texas 443.

> These state-to-state disparities exist not because people commit more heinous murders

> in California than they do in Connecticut. Rather, it is because state death penalty statutes are a patchwork of disparate standards, rules and practices that lead to different (in this case, life or death) results. It is also because some prosecutors are far more zealous in seeking the death penalty than others, particularly if they are running for election.[9]

States also have differing standards as to crimes that qualify, the age of the offender at the time of the crime, the mental capacity of the offender, and the instructions to the jury concerning alternative sentences the jury may consider. Geography should not be a factor in sentencing. If we are going to have a death penalty, we need more of a national standard.

Arguments For

Those in favor of the death penalty have a fairly compelling case. Anyone who commits a heinous crime is not fit to live in civilized society and therefore should be removed from it. As it says in the Bible, we do need to purge the evil from our midst. Admittedly, despite all the evidence to the contrary, there are still those who believe the death penalty is a deterrent keeping others from committing such offenses. However, those who admit that it is not a universal deterrent still contend that at least it is a deterrent for the individual who is executed. We have all heard stories of someone on parole, or worse yet, someone who has escaped who kills again. Obviously if they had been executed their victims would still be alive.

There are some who favor the death penalty because they believe that is the only way justice can be effectively carried out: an eye for an eye, a tooth for a tooth, etc. They believe the punishment should fit the crime, and you should pay for a life with your life. Besides, they contend, it brings closure to the victims' families.

Crimes of Passion v. Crimes of Logic

Let's be practical, the reason the death penalty is not a deterrent against murder is that most murderers do not stop and think about the consequence before they kill. Murder is not a logical crime; it is most often a crime of passion. Even when a murder is premeditated and well planned, it is still based on illogical reasoning. So, if we want the death penalty to be a deterrent, perhaps it should be for crimes in which someone makes a logical decision.

For example, white-collar crime, which devastates the lives of individuals, and in some cases, results in a suicide. Or, how about selling drugs? What if anyone convicted of selling drugs was sentenced to death unless they cooperated and provided information about their supplier; thereby, allowing the police to work their way up the drug supply chain. In a cost/benefit analysis, a few years in prison versus the chance to make a lot of money is seen as worthwhile. However, if we change the equation and use death instead of a few years in prison as the consequences, an individual may think first before committing the crime.

Or, even more important, what if we used the death penalty for those who terrorize our streets. In the year 2000, a group of terrorists killed over 16,000 Americans. That is between four and five times those killed by al-Qaida terrorists on September 11. The terrorists I am talking about are often detained, fined, and sometimes given short sentences or community service before they eventually kill. Even if caught after killing someone, they are often able to plea bargain down to manslaughter and receive a short sentence, and frequently released on parole. Naturally, I am referring to drunk drivers who use cars the same way the September 11, 2001 terrorists used planes. Admittedly drunk drivers usually do not intend to harm innocent people, but their careless disregard for the safety of the public at large has the same affect.

Would a sentence of death cause people to pause before having a few drinks and then getting behind the wheel? Obviously that is not going to happen. But, it makes as much logic as the death penalty does for any other crime.

The Means Must Justify the Ends

We all know the ends do not justify the means, but should not the means justify the ends? We must protect innocent people from the violence of those who do not hold life sacred. Innocent people can die while we are busy trying to be fair to criminals. Justice needs to be as much for past and future victims as it is for the perpetrators of crimes. We must find a way to adequately purge the evil from our midst without becoming evil ourselves. When we execute someone out of anger or a sense of revenge, we are not eliminating the "evil;" we are merely eliminating that individual. Executing murders and terrorists only gives us a self-righteous sense of satisfaction, which is un-Christian and evil in and of itself. We need to look internally to be certain our actions are not vengeful or arrogant.

If there is going to be a death penalty, it must be enacted fairly. The biblical call for there to be two witnesses before someone can be executed is really only a call to use the best available evidence. Ancient Israelites did not have DNA, or fingerprints, or any other kind of scientific or forensic evidence at their disposal. We do; therefore, we have the obligation to use everything at our disposal before putting an individual to death. And, as noted above, we must give all defendants in death penalty cases the best available legal representation.

There are some people in the world who seem to be inherently evil, who were just born that way. There are others who are so broken they cannot be fixed and because of what has happened to them as children, cannot be trusted to live in society. What should we do about these people? How do we do what is in the best interest of society without violating basic human rights? Evil is insidious; it gets into society and spreads; it is contagious and infects everyone and everything it touches. When evil has touched our lives, and our solution is to execute someone out of anger, we are merely spreading evil. At the end of the movie the Exorcist, the priest touches the girl after having been warned not to. He comes in contact with the Devil and is consumed by him. His only alternative is to jump out the window in hopes of killing the evil. If you play with fire, you will get burned. Are we as a society being burned by using the death penalty? Still, we must be certain our means justify the end results. Doing nothing in the face of evil is as bad as doing the wrong thing.

Spiritual Death

The Death Penalty as defined in the Bible can have a double meaning. There is physical death, and spiritual death. Adam and Eve did not physically die when they disobeyed God, but they did become estranged from God and suffered a spiritual death when they were cast from the Garden. In the same way, Cain did not suffer physical death for killing Abel.

> When Cain kills his brother Abel, his brother's blood cries out to God from the ground (Genesis 4:10). It is from the ground that Cain is cursed. It is the ground that "opened its mouth" to receive Abel's blood, and it is the ground that "will no longer yield to you [Cain] its strength" (4:11-12). Cain has several fears as he faces God's judgment for what he has done, and the first is

> that God has driven him "away from the soil" (4:13-14. This fear is more than a fear of losing his livelihood; his body has been cut off from it physical (and mystical) source.[10]

In other words, like his parents before him, he suffered spiritual death. The Hebrew Scriptures frequently give people a way to atone for their sins, to once again become at one with God. God does require restitution, not only to the individual harmed but also to society as a whole. Redemption for loss of life, even spiritual life could only be redeemed by the life-blood of another. Blood is life, and there is power in the blood. So God gave the ancient Israelites a series of sacrifices to atone for sin. The blood of a sacrificial animal was poured out on the altar, thereby redeeming the guilty party and paying the price for their sin.

The early Christians understood the power of the blood, and we read in Hebrews that Jesus was the sacrifice that redeems us all. The blood of Jesus was and is used to atone for our sins. He paid our debt. There is power in His blood, which was spilt on Calvary. He lost blood when beaten, when the crown of thorns was put on his head, when he was nailed to the cross, and when the soldier pierced his side with a spear. Today, His blood is spilt on the altar every time we celebrate communion. It is the blood, which has the power. He died like the lambs of old, so that we might go on living spiritually. Jesus died for you. How are you repaying that debt? He was executed in a cruel and unusual way so that we might have life and have it abundantly. How do you honor His gift to you? Think about what it means to say we are Christians. It means someone else died for us. That does not give us license to do what we please, it gives us the responsibility to live lives worthy of His sacrifice, to live as He lived with compassion for all God's children.

If Jesus died for us, redeemed us, and atoned for our sins; then He died for murders, terrorists, and other perpetrators of heinous crimes. If Jesus gave His life for them, then the debt to God has been paid. Perhaps a better option then death would be for those convicted to make restitution to the families of those they killed, and, of course, to receive a life sentence without possibility of parole ever. As a matter of fact, one survey found 55% to 60% of Americans preferred that option instead of executions.

The ancient Israelites had no other way to purge the evil than execution, but today we have prisons that can satisfy that commandment. Having spent time as a chaplain in a maximum-security prison, I wrote an article (see appendix C-4) in response to those who believe a life sentence is too lenient. In it I wrote, "Prison is not a country club life some death penalty advocates want us to believe it is. Anyone who feels prisons are too easy should be forced to spend a week in one. They would change their minds."[11]

And let us not forget the words of Jesus, Himself, when He tells Martha in the Gospel according to John, "I am the resurrection and the life. Those who believe in me, even though they die, will live, [26]and everyone who lives and believes in me will never die." (11:25b-26a). This promise was not just for Martha and Lazarus, but for all who believe in Him. "With such a declaration, Jesus abolished the death penalty of Genesis."[12]

Questions for Discussion

1. How do you feel about the death penalty? Should it be continued, or eliminated? Why?

2. If eliminate, how else can we effectively purge the evil from our midst?

3. If continue, what can we do to make the death penalty fairer in its application?

4. Is prison often a fate worst than death?

5. Can a life sentence without the possibility of parole provide the justice we seek and need?

6. What if one of the hijackers on September 11, 2001 had survived? Should he receive the death penalty?

7. What if those who hijacked the plane in Pennsylvania, had been stopped, and the plane landed safely? Should they be executed?

8. What if after all other planes were force to land, we discovered more men with the same plan? The only reason they did not succeed was they did not have time. Their intent was the same. Their disregard for human life was the same? Should they be executed? How far are we willing to go?

9. Are there crimes other than premeditated murder, which should be considered capital crimes worthy of the death penalty, or at least life in prison without the possibility of parole? What about a drunk driver who kills someone with his or her car?

10. Are your beliefs concerning the death penalty consistent with your religious convictions? If not what would you have to change to make them consistent?

Notes

[1] Martin E.P. Seligman, Ph.D., *What You Can Change & What You Can't* (New York: Alfred A. Knof, 1994) 44.

[2] D. W. Bercot, *Will the Real Heretics Please Stand Up,* (Tyler, Texas: Scroll Publishing, 1989) 105-106, (as cited on the Religious Tolerance Web Site, URL: http://www.religioustolerance.org/execute.htm.)

[3] Most Rev. Joseph A. Fiorenza, at the U.S. Catholic Conference 1999, in a list of quotes on the Religious Tolerance Web Site about Capital Punishment, http://www.religioustolerance.org/execute.htm.

[4] Sister Helen Prejean, C.S.J., in a list of quotes on the Religious Tolerance Web Site about Capital Punishment, http://www.religioustolerance.org/execute.htm.

[5] ACLU Execution Watch Web Site, http://www.aclu.org/executionwatch.html.

[6] ACLU

[7] ACLU

[8] ACLU

[9] ACLU

[10] J. Ellsworth Kalas, *Christian Believer: Knowing God with Heart and Mind – Study Manual* (Nashville: Abingdon Press, 1999) 279.

[11] Rev. James A. Nelson, "Death vs. Compassion," *The Wesleyan Christian Advocate,* (June 27, 1997) 11.

[12] Kalas, 290.

MORALITY IS IN THE EYE OF THE BEHOLDER

Suggested Scripture readings: Lev 5:1,5-6; Lev 19:10; Deut 15:11; Deut 22:1-3; Mt 18:21-22; Mt. 5:40-42; Mt 7:21-23; Mt 25:31ff; Lk 10:25-37; Lk 15:11-32; Lk 16:19-31; Lk 17:11-19; Rom 12:9-21; Rev. 20:12c.

What is Morality?

Is it moral or immoral to help someone in need? At first the answer seems obvious, but is it? Quite often one person's help is another person's hindrance. It all depends on our view of God, and what each of us believes is moral.

A greater question is not only how one individual should respond to another individual in need, but how we as a society should respond to a group of people in need? Politics and the laws subsequently enacted by those we elect affect all of society, and determine how we will carry out our responsibility to our fellow humans and consequently whether or not we are a moral nation. But first, we must answer the question, "what does it mean to be moral?"

That begs the question, "Does our religion affect our politics, or do our politics affect our view of religion and how we interpret the Bible? Or, are they both influenced by something else?" If you believe there is no God or that a god created the world, left, and therefore is no longer active in the world; then there is no after-life and every person is in it for himself or herself. Your success depends on your drive and ability. However, even if you believe God exists and is still active in the world, there are still two very distinct views a person can have of God's nature.

In his book, *Moral Politics*, George Lakoff contends the determining factor is our view of family: whether we believe in a strict father or nurturant parent model where the government functions as the parent and its citizens as children.[1] I contend that it goes deeper than that. The determining factor is whether we view God as a strict father or nurturant parent. A strict father demands obedience, personal responsibility, and accountability for our actions; a nurturant parent loves us always, forgives us when we fail, and teaches us compassion by demonstrating compassion towards us? We often refer to God as Father, the Creator, our divine parent whom we strive to imitate. So, what kind of "father" is God?

Those who believe God is a strict father see the nurturant parents as permissive and neglectful, ergo immoral. Those who believe God is a nurturant parent see the strict fathers as abusive and intolerant, ergo immoral. Consequently, one person's morality, which is based on their view of what constitutes natural law, can be seen by someone else as grossly immoral based on that person's view of natural law. Therefore, the answer to the question is it moral or immoral to help someone depends on what kind of help, and our personal view of God.

So, are there really any moral imperatives? Any morals that are just natural? Or, since we see morality through the lens of how we view God, do we therefore all see it differently? Is morality absolute, or is it variable? Does it change from culture to culture, from person to person? If so, how can we ever know what is morally correct and truly the will of God? What is the correct moral action in any given situation or set of circumstances? And more importantly, can we avoid the pitfall of moral relativism?

Strict Father Morality

If God is a strict father who demands obedience, who rewards us for good behavior, and punishes us for bad; then we should pattern our own lives and childrearing accordingly. Consequently, our view of politics and how we believe we should respond as a nation to the needs of others will be consistent with that view of God.

> Lakoff defines the strict father as someone who,
>
> ...teaches children right from wrong by setting strict rules for their behavior and enforcing them through punishment. ...He also gains their cooperation by showing love

> and appreciation when they do follow the rules. But children must never be coddled, lest they become spoiled; a spoiled child will be dependent for life and will not learn proper morals.[2]

Therefore, the government as parent should not coddle its citizens with welfare programs, affirmative action, or even student loan programs. It should severely punish those who break the rules; using prisons for retribution not reform.

We find in the Hebrew Scriptures a God who is often portrayed as a Strict Father. He is a God who demands strict obedience to His laws, rewards those who obey, and punishes those who fall away. For example, in the very beginning with the story of Adam and Eve in the Genesis, we see a God who is unforgiving and who does not give second chances. God had ordered Adam and Eve not to eat any fruit from the tree in the middle of the garden; they could eat anything else they wanted, but not any fruit from that tree. In fact, they were even forbidden to touch it. Unfortunately, they were enticed by the serpent, and ate the fruit anyway. Their eyes were opened; they became aware of the fact they were naked and they were ashamed; their innocence was lost. Adam tried to blame Eve, and Eve the serpent, but God held each of them accountable for their complicity in the sin, and punished each of them in turn.

> 22Then the LORD God said, "See, the man has become like one of us, knowing good

> and evil; and now, he might reach out his hand and take also from the tree of life, and eat, and live forever"—[23]therefore the LORD God sent him forth from the garden of Eden, to till the ground from which he was taken. [24]He drove out the man; and at the east of the garden of Eden he placed the cherubim, and a sword flaming and turning to guard the way to the tree of life. (Genesis 3:22-24)

There was no opportunity for them to redeem themselves; they were just given a sentence of death and removed from the presence of God.

During the Exodus, the Hebrews refused to enter the promise land because they were afraid. In Numbers 13, a representative from each of the twelve tribes was sent into Canaan to spy out the land. Ten of them reported, "...all the people we saw in it are of great size. There we saw the Nephilim...; and to ourselves we seemed liked grasshoppers, and so we seemed to them." (Numbers 13:32b-33) Only Joshua and Caleb gave a favorable report, and encouraged the people to follow God's command. But the people refused. For their lack of faith in God and their failure to obey God's command to enter the land, God said,

> [28]Say to them, "As I live," says the LORD, "I will do to you the very things I heard you say: [29]your dead bodies shall fall in this very

> wilderness; and of all your number, included in the census, from twenty years old and upward, who have complained against me, [30]not one of you shall come into the land in which I swore to settle you, except Caleb son of Jephunneh and Joshua son of Nun.

They then spent forty years wondering in the wilderness until all of them died before their offspring were permitted to enter the promise land. Sin has consequences. Consequently, it is moral to hold individuals in society accountable for the consequences of their own sins. In fact, it would seem the entire story of the history of the Israelites is about their being unfaithful to God, and God punishing them.

Paul says to us in 2 Thessalonians 3:10b, "Anyone unwilling to work should not eat." And, in verse 14, "Take note of those who do not obey what we say in this letter; have nothing to do with them, so that they may be ashamed." God as a strict father wants everyone to be responsible for earning his or her own way, and to only associate with others who are like-minded.

Those who are adherents of the Strict Father model believe that God is more powerful than humans; therefore, God has dominance over humans; therefore, God has moral authority over humans; therefore, God has responsibility for the well being of humans. And, they believe humans have dominance over nature, adults have dominance over children, and men have dominance over women. They see this as the natural, moral order of things; a moral order that can be expanded into race, class, and religious categories: white is better than black, rich is better than poor, Christians are better than other faith traditions (in reality the same could be said for nearly all religions, i.e., Islam is better than..., Judaism is better than..., and so forth). For Strict Father adherents, success is a sign of having been obedient and having become self-disciplined. Success is a just reward for acting within this moral system.

Nurturant Parent Morality

If we see God as a loving, caring parent who helps us and forgives us even when we do not deserve it, then we should act accordingly. Lakoff defines a nurturant parent model experience as,

> Being cared for and cared about, having one's desires for loving interaction met, living as happily as possible, and deriving meaning from mutual interaction and care. ...Children become responsible, self-disciplined, and self-reliant through being cared for and respected, and through caring for others. ...Open, two-way, mutually respectful communication is crucial. If parents' authority is to be legitimate, they must tell children why their decisions serve the cause of protection and nurtuance.[3]

Therefore, the government as parent should respect its citizens and effectively communicate its reasoning with them. Social programs should exist to meet the needs of the individual and to help them be as happy as possible. If God is a God of grace who helps people and forgives them, then the government needs to help people and give them second chances. Some problems people face are through no fault of their own. Society as a whole is responsible, and must make amends. For example, they see affirmative action not as a program, which gives someone an unfair advantage; but one that levels the playing field and removes restrictions.

Again we can learn a lot from the Bible. For example in the Hebrew Scriptures, we learn from the beginning in Genesis 1 that when God created the world, he looked around and, "saw everything that he had made, and indeed, it was very good." (Genesis 1:31b). Even in the story of Adam and Eve, before banning them from the Garden, God showed them mercy and made them clothes to wear. And, when he drove Cain away for killing his brother Abel, God put a mark on him, "so that no one who came upon him would kill him." (Genesis 4:15b). And, every time the Israelites were punished for their disobedience, God would readily forgive them whenever they cried out to him and repented. God even gives the ancient Israelites a system of sacrifices described in the book of Leviticus, which are intended to function as a means for the people to once again be at one with God.

Jesus is the ultimate Nurturant Parent. He tells us to forgive not just once, but seventy times seven times (Matthew 18:22). Jesus cared for, helped, and healed even those who did not deserve it: the story of the Good Samaritan about someone who foolish went down a dangerous road alone, the Prodigal Son who squandered all that he had and came crawling back to his father, and the cleansing of the ten lepers as reported in the Gospel of Luke of whom only one returned to give thanks. Jesus even helps some who did not ask for help, as in the story of the man with the withered hand who he healed on the Sabbath in Mark 3:1-6. Jesus never demanded anything in return, although, he would often encourage people to believe, or to go and sin no more.

The Sermon on the Mount in Matthew 5-7 contains several passages where Jesus quotes from the Hebrew Scriptures, which often had a Strict Father interpretation to them, and then would say, "But I say to you...." He would then change the interpretation into one more representative of a Nurturant Parent. At the end of Matthew we read in chapter 25:31ff that we must feed the hungry, clothe the naked, etc. The only reason we need to feed the hungry in Jesus' view is because they are hungry.

There are many other stories throughout the Gospels that are about Jesus or that Jesus tells, which demonstrate what it means to be a Nurturant Parent. All the workers in the field were paid the same wage regardless of how long they had toiled, which goes against most people's concept of fairness. Jesus forgave Peter and told him he loved him at the end of the Gospel of John even after Peter had denied him three times; a good strict father would not approve.

Jesus refused to condemn the women caught in adultery and hold her accountable for her actions; he even gave her a second chance. Jesus loved first. He modeled the behavior he wants all of us to have. Adherents of the Nurturant Parent model worship God because God loves us, not because God will punish us if we do not.

Current Issues from a Moral Perspective

When we understand that both sides of a given issue are based on the moral convictions of those who support that position, we begin to understand why politicians have so much difficulty talking to each other. However, to be effective politicians must compromise even when it involves compromising their values. If they do not, nothing will get done and the country will continue its moral decline while they debate what makes a law moral. Theologians and religionists, on other hand, must never compromise. In his book, *Gods' Name in Vain,* Stephen L. Carter warns religionists, who want to involved in politics of a lesson they all need to remember,

> Once you take sides in an electoral contest, you are stuck with your candidate, warts and all. If it turns out that your candidate actually holds positions antithetical to your religion – well, if you want to be serious about your politics, you ignore or explain away or even lie about this inconvenient fact.[4]

We need to be involved, but we must be careful. We would all be better off if we just focused on the issues, and not on electing any particular candidate or party.

The Bible frequently reminds us of our obligation to care for the widows and orphans of the world. They represented the poorest of the poor in ancient times. Today, the poor are still with us. But how we take care of them depends on our beliefs about God. Those who follow the Strict Father model believe everyone is responsible for themselves. Therefore, the poor would not be in the situation they find themselves if they would merely apply themselves more, if they would work harder, and not depend on the government or other people to take care of them. Everyone is born with the same opportunities in life, how you take advantage of those opportunities depends on how well you will do in life. Strict Fathers do not believe there are any environmental or societal conditions that keep an individual from succeeding. Giving money to the poor only encourages bad behavior, which is what got them into that circumstance in the first place. The moral thing to do is not help them, once they get hungry enough they will go out and get a job and start taking care of themselves. Besides, Strict Fathers do not believe the government should take money from those who worked hard and earned it, and give to those who are too lazy to work; that is immoral.

Those who follow the Nurturant Parent model, however, believe that society plays a major role in whether or not a person is successful. They see the need to help people who have been held down by society. They believe we must feed the poor, clothe them, educate them, and demonstrate compassion toward them; so they can become productive members of society. Nurturant Parents also believe people are born into different circumstances and have different natural abilities, which affects their ability to succeed. The moral thing to do is to help them, even if it means taking from those who have and giving it to those who do not. "From everyone to whom much has been given, much will be required; and from the one to whom much has been entrusted, even more will be demanded." (Luke 12:48b)

Another group the two sides disagree about helping are our veterans. Some men and women return from war and easily assimilate back into society. Others however, have much more difficulty making the transition. It has been said that more Vietnam veterans died of suicide and/or self-destructive lifestyles after returning home, than died in the war. Strict Fathers see these emotional problems as a sign of weakness and cowardliness. Others were able to return from war without crying about it; therefore, everyone should be able to. The Nurturant Parent has more compassion, realizes that not everyone has the same psychological make-up, and wants to offer help. Nurturant Parents acknowledge these young men and women, many who were still teenagers at the time, may have witnessed horrors, suffered horrors, and/or committed horrors no human being should ever have to endure; and therefore, should be treated with compassion not distain.

A third area where these two camps disagree concerns public education. Let's face it, most teachers fall into the Nurturant Parent camp. Teaching is a low paying, little respected profession that no right thinking Strict Father adherent would ever pursue. Being a teacher is not being successful and living up to your true potential. (This is true especially if you are a male. Teaching is a noble profession for women because it allows them to be home with their children in the afternoon and during mid-term breaks and vacations, and besides, they can then earn a little extra money for the family.) Consequently, Strict Father adherents do not want their children exposed to the morality expressed by these Nurturant Parent teachers. Plus, public school curriculum tends to teach about the warts in our history, and does not pay adequate homage to our heroes. Strict Fathers send their children to private schools where parents have input into the values and curriculum being taught. They also resent having to pay taxes for public schools when they do not receive any of the benefit from them, which is why some Strict Fathers are in favor of school vouchers. However, that is not universally true. Some parents of children currently attending private schools are against vouchers if they also go to poor children. Or, as Stephen Carter put it, they are saying,

> *Private education is fine for our children, but your children, well, they just belong ...*

> *someplace else! But not among ours! Not among the achievers, the leaders-to-be, those selected by statistics and genes and money to* **be** *the future! You go your way and we'll go ours!*[5]

Not everyone is deserving. They do not want their children threatened by undesirables being among them.

Nurturant Parents are also against school vouchers. They believe everyone should have a quality education, but they tend to believe strong public schools where no child is left behind is the best way to achieve that goal. They acknowledge that the ideal situation is one where parents are involved in their children's education, but they also realize that is not reality. Some parents cannot, or will not help their children. If we are going to break the cycle, society, via the schools, must get involved in the lives of children and insure everyone is given an equal opportunity to succeed.

Conclusion

Very few, if any, people are totally one way or the other. Most of us will take one stance on a particular issue, and will be on the other side on the next. Some people are Strict Fathers in terms of domestic issues and Nurturant Parents on foreign affairs, or vice versa. There are even a few people who are middle-of-the-road on a number of issues, and see both sides of the debate. Which in part is why it is difficult to find a politician with whom you agree totally.

Still, substantive debates on the major social issues affecting society today are not likely to occur. Both sides believe in their heart of hearts that they have the morally correct position. Each side sees the other as immoral, and a threat to the future of our nation and the world if "they" are allowed to have their way. Until there is agreement on the nature of God, the two sides will never be able to agree on anything. Consequently, as I stated above, politicians must be willing to compromise.

The Church should never compromise. There is no room for moral relativism among religious people. Theologians do not have to respect the other side's position. We can see them as just plain wrong. Religionists must do everything they can, within reason, to convince politicians to enact laws consistent with their moral principles, but theologians should never be in charge. "Religion will be at its weakest when it seems – even *seems*! – to be about partisan political advantage rather than offering answers to the great and difficult moral questions of the day."[6]

If you still believe the nation would be better off if moral, religious men were running the government, consider the Taliban of Afghanistan, or the Shiites of Iran. You may disagree with their theology and find their methods oppressive, but how would they view living in a "Christian" America? Unfortunately, morality is in the eye of the beholder.

Questions for Discussion

1. What is your view of God? Are you more of a Strict Father, or Nurturant Parent?

2. If you are more of one than the other, what are some of the issues where you take the other side?

3. Words have power. The words we use can signal in which of the two camps we belong. Do you speak of "welfare queens," or people in need?

4. Do veterans, particular homeless veterans, deserve help?

5. On what issues should the Church take a stronger stand?

6. Do government backed student loans help otherwise deserving students to get a quality education, or is it just a hand out for parents who are unwilling to accept responsibility for educating their children.

7. People get AIDS because of immoral behavior. Right or wrong? If right, should we do anything to help them; after all, a moral person would learn to say "No!"

8. Do we as a society have the responsibility to teach morality to children whose parents either

cannot or will not? If you believe the parents should be responsible, who taught the parents?

9. Can a person morally be anti-abortion and pro-death penalty? Why, or why not?

10. Do your religious beliefs differ from your political views on some of these, or other topics? If so, what would you have to change to make them consistent?

Notes

[1] George Lakoff, *Moral Politics: What Conservative Know that Liberals Don't*, (Chicago: The University of Chicago Press, 1996).

[2] Lakoff, 66.

[3] Lakoff, 108-9.

[4] Stephen L. Carter, *God's Name in Vain: The Wrongs and Rights of Religion in Politics,* (New York: Basic Books, 2000) 30-31.

[5] Carter, 155.

[6] Carter, 22.

TURN THE OTHER CHEEK? – JUSTIFIED USES OF VIOLENCE

Suggested Scripture readings:
1Sam 23:1-5; 1Sam 30:1-20; Lk 6:29;
Rom 12:19-21.

Is Violence Ever Justified?

"War! What is it good for? Absolutely nothing."[1] Or is it? War has been a part of life from the beginning of time. There has always been one group of people trying to exert control over another group of people. Most people would agree that aggressive, oppressive behavior that leads to war is unjust. However, what about those who are the recipients of that aggressive and oppressive behavior? Should they refrain from fighting back? Should they allow would be dictators and totalitarian regimes bent on world domination to win, and not fight back? Should we sit by and allow ourselves, or other innocent people to be brutalized and/or killed by tyrants, or should we act to stop them?

Sometimes violence is necessary to stop violence. The problem is, can we use violence without becoming evil? Once again, we must ask ourselves the question, "if the ends do not justify the means, do the means always justify the ends?" Is it moral to allow innocent people to suffer while we stand by refusing to lift a hand, because it may require the use of violence to stop it? Sometimes the only way to stop a deranged individual who is randomly killing people is by killing that individual. Where is the justice in seeking a humane way of stopping them if innocent people continue to be harmed? And, simply dying with the others is not a solution either. Evil people must be stopped, and unfortunately some of those people can only be stopped by violent means. Fortunately, that is not always the case; there are times when some injustices can be stopped by means of passive resistance.

Pacifism

Two noted twentieth century pacifists were Mahatma Gandhi and Martin Luther King, Jr. In their struggle for justice, they constantly urged their followers not to retaliate with violence, but to passively accept whatever beating their oppressors gave and in some cases even to die. There are causes worth dying for, which are not worth killing for.

In 1930, Mahatma Gandhi had notified the Viceroy of his plans to raid the Dharasana Salt Works. However, Gandhi was arrested before he could carry out his plans. The Indian poet, Mrs. Sarojini Naidu and Gandhi's son Manilal went ahead with the planned raid anyway. Mrs. Naidu, "warned them that they would be beaten, 'but,' she said, 'you must not resist; you must not even raise a hand to ward off a blow.'"[2] United Press correspondent, Webb Miller, was on hand, and reported the events of the day as the protestors advanced on the salt works.

> "In complete silence the Gandhi men drew up and halted a hundred yards from the stockade. A picked column advanced from the crowd, waded the ditches, and approached the barbed-wire stockade." The police officers ordered them to retreat. They continued to advance. "Suddenly," Webb Miller reported, "at a word of command, scores of native policemen rushed upon the advancing marchers and rained blows on their heads with their steel-shod lathis. Not one of the marchers even raised an arm to fend off the blows. They went down like ten-pins. From where I stood I heard the sickening whack of the clubs on unprotected skulls.[3]

They continued to come forward one column after another only to be struck down themselves. Although nothing changed legally on that day, it is regard by some as the day India became free.

Rabindranath Tagore, an Indian novelist, explained it this way, "She [Europe] is no longer regarded as the champion throughout the world of fair dealing and the exponent of high principle, but as the upholder of Western race supremacy and the exploiter of those outside her own borders."[4] Everything had changed.

According to Louis Fischer in his biography of Gandhi, "Gandhi did two things in 1930: he made the British people aware that they were cruelly subjugating India, and he gave the Indians the conviction that they could, by lifting their heads and straightening their spines, lift the yoke from their shoulders."[5]

In much the same way, Martin Luther King, Jr. opened the eyes of many Americans to the mistreatment of African-Americans, not just in the South, but throughout the nation. When the major television networks aired news footage of peaceable protestors being savagely attacked by police using clubs, dogs, and water cannons; sympathy was created for the protestors and their movement. Consequently, in a relatively short period of time numerous laws were changed and many injustices were corrected. That does not mean, of course, that we do not still have a long way to go in improving race relations.

Biblical references abound that pacifists quote to justify their position that war is never permissible. For example in the Gospel of Luke we read that Jesus said,

> "27But I say to you that listen, Love your enemies, do good to those who hate you, 28bless those who curse you, pray for those who abuse you. 29If anyone strikes you on the cheek, offer the other also; and from anyone who takes away your coat do not withhold even your shirt." (Luke 6:27-29)

Jesus is telling us not to retaliate. Paul echoes those same sentiments in Romans when he tells us, "17Do not repay anyone evil for evil, but take thought for what is noble in the sight of all. 18If it is possible, so far as it depends on you, live peaceably with all. [19]Beloved, never avenge yourselves, but leave room for the wrath of God;..." (Romans 12:17-19a). Words to live by. Right? After all, it is our duty as Christians to forgive, and love our enemies. Well, maybe.

Sadly, no matter how much we may want it to, non-violence and passive resistance only works when those it is directed towards have a moral conscience, are in a position to do something about the injustice being protested, and do not harbor a deep seated hatred for the group protesting. They may still look down on the group and feel superior to them; they just cannot out and out hate them. Consequently, when we look at a number of the unjust situations that exist today, we can see that passive resistance may not be the answer. For example, it will not work in the Palestinian-Israeli controversy, the Northern Ireland Catholic-Protestants conflict, or with the conflict between Serbs and Croats, or Serbs and Ethnic Albanians. There is too much long-standing, imbedded hatred between those groups.

In the same way, passive resistance will not work against Saddam Hussein and his mistreatment of the Kurds, or any other group he directs terrorist actions towards because he has no moral conscience. It would not have worked with Hitler and the Jews, nor will it work with Osama bin Ladin and other fundamentalist terrorist organizations.

These are people who can only be stopped by resorting to violent means. We must accept responsibility for facing evil in the world. In 1 Samuel 22:6-23,

> David models what is required in the face of evil. David takes responsibility for what has come to pass and moves toward God's future. ...The realities of evil are evident in every generation. The names of Auschwitz, My Lai, Soweto, Hiroshima, Belfast, Sarajevo, Rwanda, Mogadishu, and Selma are a partial roll call of evil in our own time. Those who would participate in the bringing of God's future cannot be those who say, "We had nothing to do with those things." God's future lies with those who, like David, say, "We are responsible.[6]

However, that does not give the United States or the rest of the world carte blanche authority to use whatever means they choose to eliminate those we consider evil. An extreme example would be dropping an atomic bomb on Iraq or Afghanistan; thereby, killing hundreds of thousands of innocent humans just to get those responsible. That would be excessive. There needs to be some restraint even in extreme circumstances. We cannot overcome evil with evil.

Just War

War is sometimes necessary and just to protect the interest of minorities. However, in so doing there should be a cost we are willing to pay. War cannot be supported or justified biblically, regardless of the need, if all we do is drop bombs (that, by the way, also kill civilian populations) hoping to bring those responsible to their knees, while simultaneously allowing them to continue abusing the very people we claim to be protecting. We need to be willing to march in and fight directly for what is right, and liberate those who need our help without contributing to their being forced to flee their homes and become refugees, whom we then refuse to support.

In Chapter 1, I referred to two stories from 1 Samuel. One was about Jonathan and his unwillingness to wait around while the enemy continued to gain strength and harass his people; therefore, he and his armor bearer attacked the Philistines camp themselves, and thereby spurred on the Israelite army. The other story concerned David and his unwillingness to cower in fear and be intimidated by the taunts of Goliath, the ancient equivalent of a schoolyard bully. Although they acted decisively and emboldened their fellow Israelites, they did not act rashly. There is a difference between bold actions and rash actions; to help individuals and governments alike distinguish between the two, theologians have been struggling over the years with developing a set of criteria for defining what, if anything, is a "Just War."

Perhaps one of the best-known theologians in recent times to struggle with this question is John Howard Yoder. In his 1984 book, *When War is Unjust: Being Honest in Just-War Thinking*, Yoder defines the criteria for a Just-War. He is a Mennonite, well known as a pacifist, and therefore against the use of any violence, at any time, for any reason. He concludes that basically the criteria can never be fully met. Still, his definitions are worth considering, especially in light of the fact there are those who contend the criteria can be met.

For a war to be just it must meet nine basic criteria, and it must meet **all** nine:

1. The authority waging the war must be legitimate.
2. The cause being fought for must be just.
3. The ultimate goal ("intention") must be peace.
4. The subjective motivation ("intention") must not be hatred or vengefulness.
5. War must be the last resort.
6. Success must be probable.
7. The means used must be indispensable to achieve the end.
8. The means used must be discriminating, both
   (a) quantitatively, in order not to do more harm than the harm they prevent ("proportionality"), and
   (b) qualitatively, to avoid use against the innocent ("immunity").
9. The means used must respect the provisions of international law.[7]

Other lists include such criteria as "announcement of intent," and an "appeal to the highest lawful authority." Regardless of the criteria used, the intent is the same: to cause moral governments to think before waging war against any enemy.

When reading the Gospels and the Letters of Paul, particular the passages quoted above from Luke and Romans, we need to remember they lived among an oppressed minority. At the very least, any war they would recommend could not meet number six "Success must be probable." The Jews of that day had no hope of overthrowing the Romans. To try would be suicide. Does that mean they would bow down and allow themselves to be abused? By no means! When Jesus turned the other cheek, he did so defiantly. He stood up to those who would oppress him. After all, they did execute him, which can happen when you take a pacifist stance.

Just Intention

Several of the criteria listed above deal with having the right intention when waging war. Obviously, wars with the intent of gaining power and control over others are not just. But neither are wars in which the primary intent is vengeance; fought in anger and a need for retaliation. Violence and war should be used only to protect the innocent and society at large from future harm. There are people who need to be stopped, not for what they did, but for what they are continuing to do or will do. Courts and civilized criminal procedures exist to take care of the evil people have done, which may mean treating those criminals more humanely than they treated their victims.

Just Proportionality

We also need to be concerned with using only the amount of force required to achieve the objective. We cannot indiscriminately kill innocent people who happen to live near the person or persons we are trying to destroy. The amount of force we use, as the criteria states, should not do more harm than the harm we are trying to stop. Even so called "smart" bombs become "stupid" on occasion and fall on unintended civilians targets; what we euphemistically call "collateral damage." Human pilots and navigators make miscalculations at times and unintentionally drop bombs on the very people they are supposed to be liberating.

As I wrote in an article during the conflict in Kosovo (see Appendix C-5), "Any cause worth killing for, ought to be worth dying for."[8]. If we are really intent on removing evil from the world, we have to be willing to commit our lives and in some cases the lives of our soldiers to the effort. We cannot accept our killing of innocent people, even for a just cause, if we are not willing to be killed ourselves. At the end of World War II, the lives of thousands of U.S. soldiers and the subsequent suffering of their families were spared when they did not have to invade mainland Japan because we dropped an atomic bomb instead. But, at what cost? Were the lives of the Japanese who died, and the suffering of their families less valuable than U.S. soldiers? Was that reasonable proportion? Similar questions can be asked about the use of Agent Orange in Vietnam, and the indiscriminate bombing of Iraq, Kosovo (including the rest of Yugoslavia), and Afghanistan. Can we say we adhered to the criteria of "just proportionality" in all those cases regardless of the ends we achieved?

We also must ask ourselves if it is justifiable to use violence against countries where American interests are at stake, i.e., oil; why is it not equally justifiable in countries which have no impact on our lives, i.e., those in Africa, Asia, and parts of South America? And, should we allow those governments that are friendly to the United States to use violence against their own people. All of which begs the question, what about the violence in our own cities: whether it is violence by the police, racial profiling, or one group of citizens terrorizing another? Do we not have the obligation to interfere there as well? And, if the violence is caused by a sense of hopelessness that people living in poverty experience, do we also have the obligation to bring them hope? In other words, we should be offering them Christ, and telling them the "good news" that Jesus is Lord.

Holy War

In an interview on the Today Show in December 2001, an Army Captain who had been wounded by friendly fire in Afghanistan referred to his profession and that of his fellow Green Berets as a "calling." I found that to be an interesting characterization. A "calling" is something we usually associate with religious occupations. However, Paul tells us in several of his letters there are a variety of gifts all given by the same Spirit. Although the gifts he lists all have to do with various aspects of the faith, why could some people not be "called" to be warriors? After all, does not society need to be protected from its foes, and other forces of evil? After all, we are not all called to preach.

Those who may be "called" to be warriors are usually the ones who win battles. They enjoy the thrill of the fight. They get excited over strategy. They study the enemy, and try to anticipate their every move. Often they are less patriotic and ideological than we think or attribute them to be. They are more interested in playing the "game" of war, than in advancing any particular cause or system of believe.

There are, however, others equally dedicated to fighting who are not "called" to be warriors in the same way. They are more concerned with fighting for the cause than they are about winning; they are the zealots. They care little about strategy and planning; they believe God will lead them, and they will be victorious because they are doing God's will. These are the ones who engage in Holy War. Holy wars have been fought for ages. The ancient Israelites waged a Holy War against the Canaanites when they were on their way to and entering the promise land. They were assisted in their endeavors by God. "...[T]ake all the people of war with you, and arise, go up to Ai. See, I have given into your hand the king of Ai, his people, his city, and his land." (Joshua 8:1b-2). Saul and David were ordained by God to lead the

Israelites in battle against their enemies. In 2 Samuel we read, [19] "David inquired of the LORD, 'Shall I go up against the Philistines? Will you give them into my hand?' The LORD said to David, 'Go up; for I will certainly give the Philistines into your hand.'" (2 Samuel 5:19)

> There have been times in history when massive force was used to accomplish a task that was perceived as being God's will. People who believe in the idea of the Holy War say that if the end result is righteous, absolute power is justified in attaining the end.[9]

The Crusades were a Holy War. Those who were waging it thought they were called by God to free the Holy Land's from the hands of the Moslems. The Inquisitions were a form of Holy War against heresy in the church and society. The Taliban sincerely believe they are waging a Holy War against Christianity, Judaism, other non-Islamic faiths, and even moderate Moslems. They believe their actions are ordained by God, and they are God's agents on earth.

As part of their Internet class for Virginia Tech entitled, "Religion in American Life," Drs. Stacey M. and J. M. Floyd-Thomas list five criteria for a "Holy War,"

1. Its cause has a transcendent validation.
2. This transcendent quality is known by revelation.

3. The adversary has no rights.
4. The criterion of last resort does not apply.
5. It need not be winnable.[10]

These criteria should scare us. Zealots do not care as much about winning, as they do about being faithful to their beliefs. As indicated in criteria number three, "The adversary has no rights." Since they are not bound by the rules of "Just War," all non-believers are adversaries; there are no non-combatants. Therefore, killing thousands of innocent people is justifiable in their minds. Terrorists, who are fighting for God, do not see themselves as terrorists, but as agents of God's will. It does not matter whether they are Moslem fundamentalists, Palestinian separatists, Irish Catholics or Protestants, members of the Aryan Nation, or some other group intent on establishing God's rule on earth. We must be careful not to become like those zealots demanding our values be shared by other nations of the world.

A Word About Forgiveness

After any tragedy, there are always those good souls who choose to forgive, so they can move on with their lives. Divine forgiveness can only be granted by God, but as individuals we need to forgive because it is good for us. Some contend we can only forgive someone if that person repents, which is putting conditions on our love and forgiveness of others. Jesus tells us, "[14]For if you forgive others their trespasses, your heavenly Father will also forgive you; [15]but if you do not forgive others, neither will your Father forgive your trespasses." (Matthew 6:14-15). If we put conditions on our forgiveness of others, we run the risk of God having conditions for our forgiveness.

The other point those who refuse to forgive miss is that forgiveness is healing for the forgiver not for the forgiven. In fact it does little for the forgiven other than perhaps to "heap coals of fire on their heads." (Proverbs 25:22). Jesus understood that, which is why he tells us to forgive not once, not seven times, but seventy times seven times. Until we let go of the anger and hatred we hold in our hearts, we will not have room for our hearts to be filled with the love of God.

That does not mean we have to forget, or even that we cannot on some level still hold those who hurt us accountable for their actions. It only means we have to let go of the hate that is eating away at our souls. Some of those we see as evil people are themselves damaged goods, tormented by demons as a result of the events in their lives. They deserve our forgiveness, perhaps even our pity, but they do not need to be able to remain among us. And, sometimes, unfortunately, we must purge the evil from our midst by means of violence.

Questions for Discussion

1. Do we have an obligation to protect the innocent? Especially those who are unable to protect themselves?

2. Review the Just War Criteria. How does it fit for any of the wars we have fought: the Revolutionary War, the Civil War, the two World Wars, Korea, Vietnam, the Gulf War, Kosovo, the battle for Enduring Freedom against terrorism?

3. Read 1 Samuel 22:22, do we have the obligation to accept responsibility?

4. How do we heed Paul's call not to repay evil with evil? Is killing innocent people, even if they are enemies, evil?

5. What if such action puts our own lives, or the lives of others in danger?

6. Are there ways other than war, especially constant bombardments for dealing with evil in the world?

7. Are there people in the world today being terrorized, brutalized, oppressed and even killed by tyrants, whom we should be protecting? In the Mid-East, in Africa, in Asia, in South America, in the United States?

8. Are your views about war and our use of our military consistent with your professed religious beliefs? If not, what would you have to change to make them consistent?

Notes

[1] From the song, "War" by Barrett Strong and Norman Whitfield, and sung by Bruce Springsteen.

[2] Louis Fischer, *The Life of Mahatma Gandhi*, (New York: Harper & Row Publishers, 1950) 273.

[3] Fischer, 273.

[4] Fischer, 274.

[5] Fischer, 275.

[6] Bruce C. Birch, "The First and Second Books of Samuel," *The New Interpreter's Bible,* (Nashville: Abingdon Press, 1998) 1149.

[7] John Howard Yoder, *When War is Unjust: Being Honest in Just-War Thinking*, (Minneapolis: Augsburg Publishing House, 1984) 18.

[8] Rev. James A. Nelson, "Something to Die For," *The Georgia Guardian*, (June 4-10, 1999) 5A.

[9] "Four Christian Views of War," by the Ministry Division of the General Assembly Council of the Presbyterian Church (U.S.A.), http://horeb.pcusa.org/kosovo/four.htm

[10] Drs. Stacey M. and J. M. Floyd-Thomas, a handout from their Internet class, "Religion in American Life." http://smft.cis.vt.edu/rel2124.

THE BREATH OF LIFE – ABORTION & EUTHANASIA

Relevant Scriptures readings: Gen 2:7; Ex 20:13; Ex 21:22; Ps 51:5; Jer 1:5; Ezek 37:1-10; Mk 10:13-16; Lk 1:39-45; Jn 14:1-3; 1Cor 15:12-19; 50-55; Phil 1:21-26.

What Then?
A day, a night; a day, a night;
And on and on they go.
One by one they slowly pass,
But always shall they flow.
But though the sun may always shine,
And the earth may always spin,
Those who walk upon the earth
Will always reach an end.
For life exists in each awhile,
And then it is no more.
But something must control the life
That comes forever more.
But where is it that we will go
When we have reached our end?
Is there a heaven, or a hell, or do we come again,
Or when live for us is over, does it simply end?
A question that each day and night

Has plagued the life of man
For when my life has reached its end,
What then, what then, what then?[1]

Questions

I wrote that poem while I was a college student in the sixties. Since that time, I have not gotten, nor has anyone else gotten, nor are we likely to get anytime soon a concise, definitive, scientific answer to that question. We humans have always wondered what happens to us after we die. Stories abound from cultures all over the world and throughout the ages detailing some type of afterlife. No one wants the party to go on without them, so we desperately want to believe that life goes on in some form or another. Plus, the belief that in an afterlife the good are rewarded and the bad punished makes it easier to accept the injustices and inequities of life in this world.

The world in the last one hundred years has gotten a lot more complicated. Today, not only do we need to worry about what happens after we die, but what constitutes death: A cessation of breathing? The heart stopping? Brain waves going flat? Or, some other determining factor yet to be discovered? And, an even more perplexing problem, when does life begin? Do we need to have breath to have life? Does the heart need to start beating? Brain waves begin registering? Does life begin simply when a sperm and an egg combine to form the cells that have the potential to develop into a human life? Or, do we in fact need a soul? And if so, what exactly is a soul? Where does it come from? Do we create one, or is the soul something given to us by God? If given by God, at what point in the development of a person does God give us a soul? And, at the end of life does a soul leave the body? If so, when? Sadly, we cannot give a concrete answer to these questions. They are simply a matter of faith that each of us must wrestle with individually. Fortunately, many of us have a fairly good idea of what is waiting for us on the other side, even if we do not know all the details.

At the end of the movie AI, the super intelligent robots, which have taken over the world, have the capacity of reconstructing a person from their DNA. If any part of a person who once lived, i.e., a piece of hair, bone, etc. can be found; they can recreate that person, talk to them, and even learn from them. Unfortunately, they found they could not recreate the "essence" of life, or the soul. Once the reconstructed person loses consciousness by falling asleep, they cannot wake up again. There is a mystical quality of life we will never be able to reproduce. We need to let God be God.

The Beginning

When does life begin? Almost everybody has an answer to that question, and depending on the answer determines his or her response to abortion. Biblically the answer is inconclusive. Admittedly, there are some who claim there is no ambiguity, but there is.

In the beginning we read, "[7]then the LORD God formed man from the dust of the ground, and breathed into his nostrils the breath of life...." (Genesis 2:7a) This would imply that Adam did not come to life until he received the Spirit of God. When the prophet Ezekiel prophesied to the dry bone in chapter 37, he tells us they did not come fully to life until, "[10]I prophesied as he commanded me, and the breath came into them, and they lived, and stood on their feet, a vast multitude." (Ezekiel 37:10) Again, life only came once there was breath in the nostrils, which is equivalent to being filled with the Spirit of God.

In Psalm 51, David is pleading with God to pardon him for his sins. He says in verse 5, "Indeed I was born guilty, a sinner when my mother conceived me." (Psalm 51:5) Some interpret this as proof life begins at conception, however that is not what the Psalm is about. The Psalms are poetry, and as such use symbolism, imagery, metaphor, and hyperbole to make a point. David is trying to say that he has always been sinful, even before he was born. If anything, this passage is more a validation of the doctrine of Original Sin, than the beginnings of life.

Jeremiah is told, "[5]Before I formed you in the womb I knew you, and before you were born I consecrated you...." (Jeremiah 1:5a) Again, this would indicate that at some point in time God forms us in the womb, perhaps that is the magical time we become human, but not necessarily at conception. The same could be said about John the Baptists who according to Luke leaped in his mother's womb upon hearing Mary's voice when she came to visit his mother, Elizabeth. (Luke 1:41). However, by the time Mary made the journey to visit them, Elizabeth was already in her sixth month making this a very compelling argument against late term abortions.

The Laws concerning violence as presented in the book of Exodus state,

> [22]When people who are fighting injure a pregnant woman so that there is a miscarriage, and yet no further harm follows, the one responsible shall be fined what the woman's husband demands, paying as much as the judges determine. [23]If any harm follows, then you shall give life for life, eye for eye, tooth for tooth, burn for burn, wound for wound, stripe for stripe. (Exodus 21:22-23)

If the unborn child was considered to be "a life," then the penalty would be a life, but the law only demands a fine. Admittedly, there are other translations, such as the King James Version, which states, "so that her fruit depart from her," instead of miscarriage. However, at the time of the King James translation any child, who was born prematurely probably died. Living would have been the exception not the rule. Therefore it seems logical to assume the addition harm referred to concerns the mother, a life, which would require a life for life, etc.

But, the mere fact the Bible does not or may not specifically define life beginning at conception is not, in and of itself, a justification for abortion at any time. Although, abortion may have been an unknown concept at the time of Christ, exposure was a common practice. Unwanted children, when born, were exposed to the elements and left to die. This seems like a cruel practice, but did those children suffer any more pain or emotional trauma than a so-called fetus in a late term abortion? Jesus says in the Gospels to "Let the little children come to me, and do not stop them." (Matthew 19:14b) Some have interpreted this story as Jesus calling for the Christian community to take in those children who are not wanted and in danger of being abandoned. At the very least it is a reminder that all life, even that of children is precious and important to God, and that they should be included in the community of believers. Also, as Christians we have the obligation to be as concerned about the rights and welfare of the children who are born as we do for those yet to be born, and to ensure all children are given a fair chance to succeed in life. Plus, it is important to remember that any system of laws which can make abortion illegal, can just as easily require abortions at some future time when it suits the needs of society to restrict the number of new births; or even more insidious, to restrict the number born of a particular race, or gender.

A secondary problem is stem cell research. If you believe life begins at conception you must be against such research because it results in the taking of a human life. We cannot justify the taking of one life to save another even if it means ending pain, suffering, and needless death. Destroying embryos to grow new cells for people who are sick or paralyzed would be the equivalent of killing young poor children who have little hope for a productive life, to harvest their organs and give them to middle and upper class children who could then have a bright, productive future. However, if you believe the cells created in a petri dish are merely a collection of cells, which have yet to develop into anything real, then you could be in favor of such research. Why allow people to continue to suffer when we have the ability to end their pain?

Like abortion, our position on stem cell research depends on our belief as to when life begins. That point in time between conception and birth that each of us believes life begins varies depending on our individual faith, and two people can come to different conclusions. But what we believe about the beginnings of life, and what makes a life a life, determines our position on other life and death issues as well.

In the Middle

Mapping the human genome, cloning, stem cell research, in vitro fertilization, in utero surgery, and genetic engineering are all scientific capabilities that biblical writers never conceived of. We justify all of these advances and additional research with the best of intentions. Our goal and that of the scientists involved in these projects is to ease the pain and suffering of others. We want to help infertile couples to have children, we want children to be born without birth defects, and we want people who suffer from incurable diseases to be cured. All noble goals.

However, there are others who will in time find a way to use the results of this research for their own evil purposes and to advance their own agendas. All of these topics relate in some way or another to our understanding of the essence of life. We are constantly learning more and more about the building blocks of life, and what makes a person a person. Once a certain element in society learns how to control those building blocks of life, there is no stopping how they will be used. Genetic engineering, for example, will allow those so inclined to at least attempt to create a super race. Other equally catastrophic consequences could result even from what appears to be legitimate purposes.

The human body has shown amazing resilience over the centuries and an ability to adapt naturally to the ever-changing environment. How will our interfering in the natural genetic evolutionary process affect how humans continue to adapt in the future? We just do not know what the long-term affects of interfering with genetics may be. We run the risk of removing genes from the gene pool, which could be essential for humans several generations from now to survive. Or, we could be helping defective genes further infect the gene pool leading to catastrophic consequences in the future. What if the children we help come into being from infertile couples, or the pregnancies we help to go full-term that would otherwise have resulted in a miscarriage are carrying genes, which God and nature wanted to keep out of the gene pool? In fact 16-20% of all known pregnancies end in miscarriages, and many more undetected pregnancies end in the first month. Some researchers put the total number of miscarriages as high as 40-50% for all conception. Pregnancies usually fail because something is wrong with the child. What is moral about bringing potentially deformed children to life? Are we not in fact keeping people alive whom nature wanted dead? That is something we will not know the answer to until hundreds of years in the future, perhaps after it is too late. So the question becomes, if it is wrong to kill a life God wanted to live, is it not also wrong to keep alive a life God wanted to end? Obviously, these are not easy questions to answer.

While attending the University of Oxford Summer Programme in Theology, I wrote an essay on this subject for a class called, "The Ethics of Creation." The essay began with this short story,

> She awoke to the dawn of a new day. The sun was out; temperatures were expected to reach 150°. Her thick, dark skin protected her from the ultra-violet rays of the sun, which had killed off the Homo sapiens. The membrane covering her nose helped her to filter out the harsh pollutants in the air. Her lungs were able to breath the air because of a rare disease a former life

form had failed to eradicate. The year was 3127.

Prior to the establishment of her species, the earth had gone through 1000 years of suffering. The humanoids that populated the earth had evolved several centuries earlier from the Homo sapiens, though there were some who still refused to believe it despite the evidence. This new species of humanoids were continuing to adapt to the constantly changing environment.

Some of their scientists were saying they only existed because of a discovery made in the year 2075. The geneticists of that age had perfected, or so they thought, gene therapy. They had eliminated most of the diseases in the world. They had slowed the aging process allowing people to live well beyond 150 years. Unfortunately, the population grew out of control. Global warming, lack of natural resources like palatable water, and air pollution began killing the people. The destruction of the O-zone layer allowed ultra-violet light through which led to skin cancer. The pollution was so bad people couldn't breathe.

In 2075, a scientist noticed children with cystic fibrosis, those few who were left, were actually helped by the pollutants in the air. After further research, she discovered the build-up in their lungs from the

> disease actually allowed them to breath the air. Suddenly, scientists began genetically altering everyone to have cystic fibrosis. Only those with the disease had offspring who survived. Fortunately, the Homo sapiens had not eliminated it or there would be no intelligent life on earth.[2]

Obviously this is pure fiction, but it does point out the fact we have no idea what the results of genetic engineering may be.

Ethical questions arise as we learn about genetics, and the effect of genes on behavior. What are the implications of behavioral genetic research on society? We will have to deal even more often with the ethical dilemma of the nature v. nurture controversy. "What social consequences would genetic diagnoses of such traits as intelligence, criminality, or homosexuality have on society? What effect would the discovery of a behavioral trait associated with increased criminality have on our legal system? If we find a 'gay gene,' will it mean greater or lesser tolerance?"[3] Will this lead to a fatalistic view of life in which we excuse bad behavior in others, and justify our own actions as being inbred and not something we can control? What will this view of life say about our doctrine of "free will"? Besides, then we would have to totally exclude all environmental influences as irrelevant, and all social programs to make life better for people would become superfluous.

Logically, it would seem that genetics would be a factor, but not the only factor in determining a person's behavior and their personality. We cannot rely solely on genetic research to solve or even explain the problems of society. A BBC News report states, "Researchers are predicting that the data will unlock some of the secrets of how genes influence behaviour [English spelling]. But they warn against headline-making claims that a given gene can be the cause of crime, homosexuality or even sporting brilliance."[4] A person's environment will continue to be seen as a major factor in their personality and behavior. For example, the Danish study I quoted in Chapter 2 found that about one-third of those whose parents were criminals, and who were raised by criminals became criminals themselves.[5] However, that also means that two-thirds do not. Two-thirds are able to overcome both nature and nurture and lead productive lives.

Dr. Craig Venter, a leader in the effort to decode the human genome, was quoted in that same BBC News story saying that because of environmental influences, "'you can't have Xerox copies of people; you can't have clones of people that will be the same.'"[6] That will be good news to most people, and bad news to a few.

The End

Although we cannot definitively define when life begins, we think we know when life ends. But, do we? What constitutes the end of life? In the past, it was when a person stopped breathing. As science learned more about life, it became when their heart quit beating. However, today we can keep a person breathing and their heart beating indefinitely. Therefore, we depend more on brain waves, but even those are not totally conclusive. We cannot determine exactly when a soul enters a body, nor can we be sure when it leaves, if it leaves. As Christians we "believe in the resurrection of the body," which implies the body and the soul are inseparable. A fact, which only further complicates things. Consequently, those are questions we cannot easily answer, so let us look at what we can discuss.

Why are we so obsessed with death? Paul was not afraid to die, he even looked forward to dying, "[21]For to me, living is life and dying is gain. [22]If I am to live in the flesh, that means fruitful labor for me; and I do not know which I prefer. [23]I am hard pressed between the two: my desire is to depart and be with Christ, for that is far better; [24]but to remain in the flesh is more necessary for you." (Philippians 1:21-24). Paul knew what awaited him on the other side; he knew he was destined for eternity with Christ, and long for it. Although, he also knew his work here on earth was not quite finished.

If as Christians, we truly believe in eternity with God, why would we do anything to delay that event? Of course, there is no reason to hasten that day, we should allow nature to take its course, and let our life end when our work here is through. How many souls, which are longing to go home, do we keep trapped in bodies lying lifeless in nursing homes? Why keep alive a body, which has lost all quality of life? Of course, that raises another question: Can we justify ending a life that has lost all quality of life? Like abortion, our view of euthanasia depends on what we believe is the essence of life.

Putting life above everything else can have other consequence as well. Jesus tells us to take up our crosses if we want to follow him; in other words, we must be willing to die for what we believe is truly important. "For those who want to save their life will lose it, and those who lose their life for my sake will save it." (Luke 9:24) When we seek to save our lives at all costs, we risk damaging our souls. How often does our fear of dying get in the way of our being able to do the work and will of God in the world, and to be true disciples of Jesus Christ? As Martin Luther King, Jr. said, "If a man has not discovered something that he will die for, he isn't fit to live."[7]

Life on earth is temporal. It was always so. In the beginning, in the creation story in Genesis, Adam and Eve were removed from the Garden of Eden before they had the opportunity to eat of the tree of life and live forever. At that point in time they were not immortal, and God wanted to ensure they did not become immortal. Death is natural, and we all must eventually leave this world to make room for the next generation. Without death, life has no meaning anyway. In *Gulliver's Travels* by Jonathan Swift, in the Kingdom of Luggnagg, there was a group known as the Struldbruggs or the Immortals, who are born with a red spot on their foreheads, which later turned green, then blue, and finally black. Gulliver's initial reaction was that it would be wonderful to live forever, to have time to study all the arts, and to gain immense knowledge. However, after he finished extolling all the virtues of immortality, he was told the reality: these men and women were miserable for they still grew old and feeble. "[W]henever they see a funeral, they lament and repine that others are gone to a harbour of rest, to which they themselves never can hope to arrive."[8] They long for a death they can never have. The Struldbruggs teach us longevity without quality of life is not something to be desired.

The Essence of Life

When does life begin? When does life end? What constitutes life? All questions which for now are better answered by faith than by science. But whatever we believe is that special quality which gives life life, it will determine our opinion on a wide range of other issues as well. We cannot change our view when it suits us, either something is alive and should be held sacred, or it is not. The important thing is to remain consistent in our beliefs.

Questions for Discussion

1. When does life begin?
2. When does life end?
3. What words to you use in reference to the unborn? Child? Fetal matter? Baby?
4. What do the words people use tell us about their beliefs?
5. What is your view of stem cell research? Are we killing a potential human, or are we merely using a collection of cells to help others?
6. Can we justify taking one life to save another?
7. Did we live before? Will we live again?
8. Should we allow people to die when they feel their time on earth is through, and their work is done? Should we allow doctors to help the terminally ill die, particularly if the only reason they are alive is because of medical treatments in the past?
9. Should we actively help people die who are no longer able to make decisions for themselves?
10. Should we keep people alive at great expense if the same money could be used to save hundreds of others from lives of suffering?

11. Has your fear of dying ever gotten in your way of doing ministry in the world? Of, picking up your cross and following Jesus? If so, when and how?

Notes

[1]Jim Nelson, A collection of poems, 1967.

[2]Jim Nelson, "A Look Into the Future," 2000.

[3]United States Government "Human Genome Project Information" web site, http://www.ornl.gov/hgmis/elsi/behavior.html.

[4]"Nature or Nurture," BBC News web site, http://news.bbc.co.uk/hi/english/sci/tech/newsid_1164000/1164792.stm.

[5]Martin E.P. Seligman, Ph.D., *What You Can Change & What You Can't* (New York: Alfred A. Knof, 1994) 44.

[6]"Nature or Nurture."

[7]Martin Luther King, Jr., from a speech in "The Speeches Collection: Martin Luther King, Jr." (MPI Home Video, 1990).

[8]Jonathan Swift, *Gulliver's Travels*, (Garden City, N.Y.: Doubleday and Company, Inc., 1945) 214.

TEACHING THE CHILDREN & SCHOOL PRAYER

Relevant Scriptures are Gen 1:1-2:3; Ex 12:26-27; Deut 4:9-10; Deut 6:4-9; Deut11:18-21; Josh 24:14-15.

Tell Your Children

"And when your children ask you, 'What do you mean by this observance?' you shall say...." (Exodus 12:26-27a) God tells the Israelites they must teach their children about their religious observances. The only way future generations will know the significance of Passover, or any other celebration is if the current generation teaches them. At other times God simply tells them, "You shall tell your child...." (Exodus 13:8a). You cannot always wait for them to ask the questions; sometimes you just have to tell them.

God knew the importance of teaching the children in order to keep the faith alive. But at the same time, God also knew that in teaching we learn. Anyone who has ever taught, whether in the school systems, at their place of work, or in Sunday school knows the truth of that statement. Therefore, it is equally important for us to teach the children for our own edification as it is for theirs. We gain a new and deeper understanding of the truth of the faith when we endeavor to explain it to our children. In Deuteronomy God tells us, "But take care and watch yourselves closely, so as neither to forget the things that your eyes have seen nor to let them slip from your mind all the days of your life; make them known to your children and your children's children." (Deuteronomy 4:9). Retelling the story also helps us to remember, and not to forget the saving grace of God.

The problem comes with what we teach, and how we teach. Do we merely have our children memorize facts and biblical verses, or do we encourage them to look beneath the surface of the words to the truth of the story. In the passage from Exodus quoted above, God was telling the Israelites to tell their children how God had delivered them from the hands of the Egyptians. The important part was not so much the details of what happened, but the fact that God was involved in their salvation and, "so that you may know that I am the LORD." (Exodus 10:2b) That is a message of hope, which must have been of great comfort years later to the exiles in Babylon.

Today, like then, it is more important for us to teach our children about the saving grace of God, then the facts of the story. The story is merely a tool to help them understand by giving them an example of the doctrine of salvation in worldly terms. If we are not careful, we run the risk of making the words more important than the meaning. That would be a form of idolatry: worship of the literalness of the Bible instead of the truth God wants us to know.

It is also important to encourage our children to ask questions. God made us to be curious, and so God fully anticipated the children would ask, as noted in the quote at the beginning of this chapter. Of course children can be infuriating when they ask too many questions, which is why we often respond with, "because I said so." But God wants us to struggle with the answers, particularly when it comes to questions of faith. For our faith grows when we teach it to our children, or for that matter to those who are children of the faith. Oddly enough, sometimes the questions we ask and our struggles with them are more important than the answers we receive.

We also have to be careful about what we teach. The words we use, the messages we give can have drastic, long-lasting effects. We teach more by what we do than by what we say. In the movie *Malcolm X* by Spike Lee, a teacher responds to a young Malcolm's essay about wanting to be a lawyer when he grew up, that it is not a realistic goal for Negroes, and maybe he should consider being a carpenter, or some other occupation using his hands.[1] The problem is children believe the lies we tell them. As intelligent as Malcolm X was, imagine what he may have become had he been given the support and the opportunity others were given. Could he have been a lawyer the caliber of Thurgood Marshall, and brought about what would have been perceived as positive changes to society? Children are impressionable; we must be honest and supportive with them, and give them every opportunity to succeed in life.

All of which begs the question, then who should teach? James tells us, "Not many of you should become teachers, my brothers and sisters, for you know that we who teach will be judged with greater strictness." (James 3:1). Not everyone should be a teacher. Too many churches make someone a Sunday school teacher without giving them any training or ensuring they have any legitimate knowledge of theology or the Bible. This only perpetuates a lot of myths and untruths about the stories in the Bible and their meaning, which can lead innocent children, as well as adults, down the wrong path. Sunday school teachers should be as qualified in their subjects as teachers in regular schools. Sunday school teachers should also be required to attend classes themselves: educational theory, formal Bible studies such as *Disciple Bible Study*, theology courses like *Christian Believers*, and denominational studies which will ensure they have at least some grounding in the beliefs of the denomination with which they are associated.

School Prayer

A debate has raged in recent years about whose responsibility it is to teach the children about moral behavior. Some actually want schools to teach morality? But, if they do that, on what religion will it be based? The United States, like it or not, is a pluralistic society. Most of the religions of the world are practiced by our citizens. So who will be teaching morality, and based on what theology? Do we really want just any teacher, regardless of their theology, teaching religion or praying with our children?

As part of an article entitled, "State-sponsored Prayer Erodes Religious Freedom," which I wrote for the *Georgia Guardian* (see Appendix C-6) in response to a group advocating a constitutional amendment allowing school prayer, I included a sample prayer I was sure would be approved by the courts. It goes,

> Divine and/or Supreme Being or beings who may or may not exist, and who may or may not have created the universe; we pray, or perhaps we just say that we are grateful for this day, and for our school. We hope that we will be able to learn, that we will respect the property of school, that we will be kind to our teachers and to one another, and that we will not resort to violence. The end.[2]

I the went on to say in that same article that

> [w]riting a school prayer that will be acceptable to Christians, Jews, Muslims, Hindus, Buddhists, as well as Mormons, Branch Davidians, Heaven's Gaters, and of course atheists will be impossible. A nation built on the concept of Religious Freedom cannot suddenly change and force a particular belief on everyone's children. Trying to pass such a law will only point out religious in-

> tolerance, and in the end do more harm than good."[3]

Eventually, "The only prayer that will ever be approved will be so watered down, most people will ask, 'What's the point?' The problem is that in their attempts to offend no one they will offend everyone."[4] Can any of us honestly say, that is the type of prayer we want our children to learn?

Besides, children have always had, and still have the right to pray in school, before school, or any other time they choose, so long as they do not interfere with the rights of others. But perhaps the most important place for children to learn to pray is in the home. If people want their children to spend time in prayer everyday, they should set the example and pray with them.

Freedom is something we lose one incremental step at a time. Once we allow government to decide what is a legitimate prayer, we begin losing our freedom of religion. A prayer we as Christians agree with today can easily be changed by a newly elected government in the future into a prayer we do not agree with. We may even find ourselves as Christians in the minority. Be careful what you pray for, you may just get it. State sanctioned prayer is just the first-step down the road leading to the erosion of our religious freedom. We need to stop looking to the government to raise our children for us, and stop abdicating our rights and responsibilities. If you want your children to pray, teach them yourself, and set a good example by praying with them in the morning before sending them off to school.

Even more disastrous results can come from religious teaching in the public schools. In 1999, the Georgia Board of Education was asked to vote on whether or not to include "Bible I" and "Bible II" in the list of approved courses for public schools. Proponents of the courses claimed they would not be religion classes, but that schools would merely be teaching the Bible as history with no mention of God, or creation. That is impossible. "You cannot teach anything about the Bible without referring to God. After all, the whole Bible is about our relationship as humans with the Divine."[5] Besides, if you are (insert your religion here) and your child's teacher is a (insert a faith or denomination you disagree with here) do you really want them giving your children religious instruction?

Who is Responsible?

So who should be responsible? The obvious answer is the parents. But what happens when the parents are unwilling or unable to teach their children? Do we just let those children fall through the cracks?

The hope is that good Christians everywhere will accept responsibility for teaching the children. In the Baptismal Liturgy of the United Methodist Church, the congregation pledges to nurture one another in Christian life, especially those who are being baptized, "We will surround *these persons* with a community of love and forgiveness, that *they* may grow in *their* trust of God, and be found faithful in *their* service to others."[6] That congregation is accepting on behalf of Christians everywhere the responsibility to help those persons being baptized grow in the faith as others accepted the responsibility on our behalf; thereby, making all Christians responsible for the moral upbringing of one another, and especially for the religious education of the children. Because, when we are baptized and become part of the community of faith we give the other members of the community, or parents give on behalf of their children, the right to interfere in our lives to ensure we grow in our faith, and are true to the principles of Christianity. Of course when we are the ones exercising that right we need to do so in a loving, compassionate, Christ-like manner.

To fully succeed in the world and be faithful Christians, people also need to be educated in other subjects as well. If a child cannot read, how can they read the Bible, and come to know and understand the Word of God? Therefore, as good Christians it is important for us to "teach" the children. Again, we cannot rely on the schools to do everything, nor can we depend on parents since too many of them cannot or will not work with their children. "The public schools are not staffed to handle the number of students who need special attention and assistance in learning the basics. Volunteers, and paid staff in churches are capable of doing just that. They can give the one-on-one attention many of these young children need to give them a competitive chance in the world."[7] Churches can do what other segments of society cannot, with or without government funding. Plus, since the tutoring is going on in a church, and the parents have agreed to allow their children to attend, the church can teach morality and religion at the same time. It is just as easy to learn reading from a religious text as it is from a secular one. All churches need to be more involved in their communities.

What Do We Teach?

Do we teach the good with the bad? Let's face it all history is revisionist history. Like the Evangelist tells us at the end of John about the various things relating to the life of Jesus, "if every one of them were written down, I suppose that the world itself could not contain the books that would be written." (John 21:25b) What is left out a book can be as important and tell us as much about the beliefs of the writer as what is included. There is not enough time or space to convey all knowledge from history. For example, do we teach the violent passages in the Bible, and the violent periods of church history: The book of Judges, the Crusades, the Inquisitions, etc.? Or, do we only teach what we want the next generation to know about. Whether our history is viewed as noble or shameful depends on the facts, and how they are presented. Can we trust children, or anyone for that matter, to hear the truth about our past?

When we overly idealize something it loses its significance and becomes more of a fairy tale than truth. Teaching the bad with the good, reminds us that even our heroes are human. Seeing the warts can make the contributions they made seem even more spectacular. The mere fact that Christianity survived despite the Crusades and the Inquisitions is a testament to the actions of God in the world, and the resilient of the faith. Christianity is big enough, and significant enough to withstand the scrutiny of those who only want to view the negative. As Jesus tells us, "Nothing is covered up that will not be uncovered, and nothing secret that will not become known." (Luke 12:2) Jesus is telling us we may as well admit the truth, the whole truth, even that which is uncomfortable for us. Like in politics, it is not the action but the cover up that will get you. If we cannot hide the truth, why try? Plus, people become disillusioned later if they feel they have been misled or lied to. It would be as though we were putting stumbling blocks before the little ones who believe, and you know what that will lead to. (Mark 9:42)

Public Education

Conservatives do not like public education. They feel that it has lost its moral compass. As noted in Chapter 3, some people view God as a Strict Father and others as a Nurturant Parent. Nurturant Parents are more service oriented, while Strict Fathers are success oriented. Teaching is seen primarily as a service occupation. Teachers are not viewed as "successful" by worldly, financial standards. Consequently, those in education are more likely to teach students "Nurturant Parent" morality, and have what appears to be a more lenient manner of working with problem children.

According to Martin Marty, "Liberal disruption shows up in primary and secondary schools, especially in the areas of sex education and social commentary."[8] Those are exactly the areas conservatives worry about the most. Marty goes on to say that in the public school system conservatives believe,

> liberals tend to acquiesce in the idea that they cannot prevent all teenagers from having sex, so they promote health causes, such as the counsel to use condoms. They might want to advance the notion that homosexual lifestyles are acceptable. They teach not a well-defined set of moral truths but "values clarification." All these are abhorrent signs of liberal incivility to their opponents. These foes see liberals as having sneaked or forced their way into positions from which they can propagate their ideas and subvert systems.[9]

Consequently, true conservatives send their children to private schools where they can have a lot more say about the curriculum and the values taught. "Indeed, one of the strongest arguments in favor of public assistance for private school tuition is that only in that way can parents choose for themselves the education their children should have, rather than having some other entity, one over which they may have little control, make choices for them."[10] For example, parents want to decide whether they can, "on religious grounds, exempt their children from sex education, some parts of biology or history, or condom distribution programs."[11] As Stephen Carter notes, far too many of these disputes with public education end in litigation.

Conservatives also do not like Nurturant Parent teachers because, "Nurturant Parent moral views subverts traditional morality just because it teaches children to think for themselves and not just obey authority."[12] This contributes to the rise in animosity towards liberal education, which was the mainstay of the sixties. More and more young people are encourage to follow a structured course of study leading to a financially rewarding career.

The debate over who is responsible for public education, the parents or the so-called experts, will continue to wage for years to come. Too much parental influence can have drastic affects on minorities when a majority of a community is of the same faith. At the same time, too much influence by educators causes parents to feel alienated from their children's education, and could result in the loss of public education. Ultimately, we must decide what is in the best interest of the child and what is in the best interest of society at large.

One last caveat, even though religion may not belong in the public schools, there should not be hostility toward religion either. Although we cannot and should not depend on the school systems to teach our children about morality, we should not be afraid they will be taught immoral behavior either.

Questions for Discussion

1. What myths about the Bible and/or religious history were you taught as a child? How did you feel later when you learned the truth?

2. How should we teach about the violence in the Bible?

3. What should be the qualifications to teach any Sunday school class?

4. What aspect of our history are we not teaching in the schools? What should we be teaching?

5. Does it really take a village to raise children? If so, who are our neighbors?

6. What biblical stories should we NOT teach children?

7. Does sex education encourage or discourage sex among teenagers? Should we teach birth control methods other than abstinence?

8. How can your church help students to learn?

9. What can we do to make public education better?

Notes

[1]Spike Lee & Arnold Perl, *Malcolm X,* a Spike Lee movie, Warner Brothers, 1992.

[2]Rev. James A. Nelson, "State-sponsored prayer erodes religious freedom," *The Georgia Guardian*, (June 19-25, 1998) 5A.

[3]Nelson

[4]Nelson

[5]Rev. James A. Nelson, "Keep government out of religion," *The Georgia Guardian,* (August 20-26, 1999) 3A.

[6]"The Baptismal Covenant I," *The United Methodist Hymnal*, (Nashville: The United Methodist Publishing House), 35.

[7]Rev. James A. Nelson, "Funding faith-based afterschool programs," *The Georgia Guardian*, (September 18, 1999) 4A.

[8]Martin E. Marty, with Jonathan Moore, *Politics Religion and the Common Good*, (San Francisco: Jossey-Bass Publishers, 2000) 37.

[9]Marty

[10]Stephen L. Carter, *The Culture of Disbelief*, (New York: Basic Books, a Division of Harper Collins Publishers, 1993) 170.

[11]Carter

[12]George Lakoff, *Moral Politics: What Conservatives Know that Liberals Don't*, (Chicago: The University of Chicago Press, 1996), 242.

APPENDIX A

Suggested Class outline for using this book as a six week study

1. Ensure everyone has a copy of the book, or access to one when advertising the class. Encourage them to read each chapter before each session.

2. Open each session with an appropriate prayer.

3. Read the selected biblical text or texts. Add any you feel appropriate.

4. Read a saying or quote on the subject from other sources, especially if you can find something spiritual.

5. Ask the class to define the issues being study, and to suggest questions for discussion.

6. Give a brief overview of the material contained in this book. Add any information or ideas you may have.

7. Give a brief commentary on the biblical passage(s) selected.

8. Ask questions for discussion from the end of each chapter, and address those raised by the

class at the beginning of the session. Encourage the class to defend their positions by using scripture or traditional religious beliefs. Focus the discussion, as much as possible, on the consistency of each individual's religious and political convictions.

9. Introduce the topic for the next session.

10. Close with a prayer.

APPENDIX B

SECOND TUESDAYS

Another suggestion to help churches get involved in discussing the issues important to society today is to invite experts in various fields to speak. The purpose of these programs is to discuss the intersection of the moral and political aspects of the issue being presented. The format would be similar to a talk show with a moderator, who introduces the topic and the speaker, allows the speaker the opportunity to make an opening statement, then asks clarifying questions, and finally calls on members of the audience to ask questions. These events could be held monthly, say on the Second Tuesday, for example, which is the reason for the name, or at any other time, i.e., First Wednesdays, Fourth Mondays, etc. Or, they could be part of the program for Family Night Dinners once a month. Find what works best for your church.

Some possible topics follow:

Person	Possible Topics
Politicians	The role of Religion in Politics
	The morality of certain legislatively enacted laws: Faith Based Initiatives
Lawyers & Judges	The morality of getting the guilty off & other moral dilemmas.
	Supreme Court decisions

Lawyers & Judges	The morality of some laws
Doctors	Bio-ethics
	End-of-life measures: allowing people to die vs. assisted suicide
	Who lives and who dies? Affordable/ reasonable health care
Teachers or members of the School Board	The place of religion in the Public Schools
	School Prayer
	Religion classes, i.e., teaching the Bible in public schools
	Creationism vs. Evolution
	Teachers' rights to express religious beliefs
Artists	N.E.A. & public funding of objectionable art

When you ask someone to come and speak, make sure you tell them they will be asked hard questions and be put on the spot. Let them know the discussion will revolve around the morality of the issue: Why is it good for society? Why do we need what they are advocating? As well as, who gets hurt? Is it a zero sum game? Or, does everyone benefit? Or, only a few selected people? Try not to get too personal, but still force those speaking to morally defend their positions.

Encourage those attending the lectures to learn as much as they can about on the subject being discussed in preparation for attending the event.

APPENDIX C-1

This article first appeared in the
Wesleyan Christian Advocate
December 6, 1996

Contrary to Conventional Wisdom

By Jim Nelson

Conventional wisdom tells us that the two subjects we should always avoid in social settings are religion and politics. Since I write a column where these two intersect, you can imagine some of the discussions I have. However, these two subjects need to be discussed, and they need to be discussed together.

As a nation, we have tried to keep them apart by developing a doctrine referred to as "separation of church and state." This is a modern concept invented by people who don't like the church telling them how to think. The First Amendment was written to protect religion from government, but we have turned it around in our attempt to protect government from religion.

Many people even try to use this doctrine in their personal lives. We are a nation that wants to compartmentalize everything. We want to have our religious self, our political self, our work self, our recreation self. We do not want one interfering with the others. But life does not work that way. We are who we are. We cannot separate our various selves into different compartments. There is no separation of faith and politics on a national level or a personal one.

Our core beliefs affect everything we do. We cannot want the church to act one way and society in general to act a different way. What we do on Monday is what we really believe, not what we say on Sunday. We need to hold ourselves, each other, and our government accountable for our actions. We need to look at and understand the theological implications of political actions.

When we are demanding that the government take action on a specific problem, we need to ask ourselves honestly, "What would Jesus do in this situation?" Then, we should decide if our political beliefs are in agreement with our religious beliefs and, if not, which ones are we going to change? What is really important to us? Are we a nation under God, or, as some people say, a "nation under gold"?

We have the obligation to discuss the issues of life, to fully understand them. To do that, it is important to read and to talk with people with whom we disagree. The truth usually lies somewhere in the middle.

If we only talk with those who agree with us, we do not grow. The only way to make the right decisions in life is to look at all sides of issues and pray about them.

The Hebrew Scriptures are full of stories about kings and advisors to kings. One reason Jesus was crucified was that he upset the political stability of the day and threatened the political power of the religious leaders. Like the prophets of old, we need to advise our political leaders and, like Jesus, we need at times to threaten the political establishment. Take every chance you get to discuss religion and politics.

APPENDIX C-2

This article first appeared in the
Wesleyan Christian Advocate
March 12, 1999

Compartmentalizing Our Faith

By Jim Nelson

A word that came into fashion as a result of the scandals surrounding the president and his subsequent impeachment is "compartmentalization." People were amazed that President Clinton seemed able to compartmentalize his personal and professional lives. The scrutiny, the embarrassment and the pressure he was under during the entire ordeal might have caused someone else to crumble, but Clinton stayed strong and continued to function as president.

I wonder if it is really a good thing to compartmentalize our lives. Or for that matter, can we? What we value will always surface in our actions. The only way the president could carry on would be if, at his innermost core, he believed what he did was acceptable. We cannot and should not compartmentalize our basic core values from the rest of our lives. What we profess on Sunday morning cannot be separated from how we conduct business on Monday morning, how we vote on Tuesday, or how we behave on Friday and Saturday nights. We are what we are.

Admittedly, I found it difficult to support the impeachment of the president based on the charges that were brought. Had the impeachment been solely for his immoral sexual conduct, I would have been in favor of it. But the House members' inability to deal honestly with that issue forced me to question their values and their motives in bringing the charges.

There were groups I felt should have been more in favor of impeachment. For example, why were feminists not more incensed by the president's behavior? Why didn't they demand his resignation for what was clearly improper sexual conduct with a female subordinate who was obviously in an unequal power relationship? Perhaps they supported the president because he supported their causes, helped push through legislation they favored and vetoed some they opposed. But isn't that selling out for political gain? What are their real core values if they are willing to turn a blind eye to an abuse of power over a woman?

And what about the American people in general? Would Clinton have gotten the same level of support had the economy been in shambles? Is everyone willing to look the other way when they believe a greater good can be achieved by doing so? Are we willing to sacrifice our values for a little gain? Doesn't this place us on the proverbial slippery slope? How much is our moral compass worth? Did we, the American people, try to "compartmentalize" our beliefs by separating them from our wallet?

We need to reorient our national compass. Otherwise, where will we be at the end of time? Will we be like those at the conclusion of the Sermon on the Mount who Jesus says only profess the word and cry out, "Lord, Lord," thereby building their faith on a foundation of the shifting sands of secularism? Or will we be like those who build on a foundation of rock; those who hear the word and do the will of our Father in heaven in all aspects of our lives – not just when it is convenient?

APPENDIX C-3

This article first appeared in the
Wesleyan Christian Advocate
March 17, 2000

In Praise of Extremists

By Jim Nelson

Last month I called on everyone to vote. I felt the nominee for both parties would be determined on March 7, and we in Georgia would have a say in that decision. I strongly believe it is important for Christians to remain active in the political process. How we vote is a reflection of our core beliefs, and of the depth of our convictions.

Consequently, I was a little disturbed by Sen. John McCain's remarks about the involvement of religious extremists. He made a speech in which he said, "Neither party should be defined by pandering to the outer reaches of American politics and the agents of intolerance whether they be Al Sharpton or Louis Farrakhan on the left, or Jerry Falwell or Pat Robertson on the right." Although I agree that neither party should be defined by them and that the "agents of intolerance" should not be the dominant voice, I do believe they should be included. Both parties need to be tolerant enough to include the intolerant.

Besides, we need people like those McCain mentioned to keep the rest of us honest. They bring important issues to the table, and keep them in the public debate. Issues those candidates running in the middle would just as soon not talk about. Those extreme men and women with passion, who hold strongly to their convictions and who believe that only their position is the right one, force the rest of us to justify our own beliefs politically and theologically. Let's face it; on most issues there really is no middle ground. Either you believe in something or you don't. Consequently, politics and religion do belong together whether we like it or not.

Take abortion for example. Most candidates would prefer not to take a firm stand because the basic question that must be answered first is theological: When does life begin? If you believe in the sanctity of life and that the unborn is a life and therefore has equal rights and protections under the law, then you must be pro-life; unless of course you favor the death penalty. Because, if you acknowledge society has the right to establish criteria which determines when it is acceptable to terminate a life, then you must be pro-choice. You can't have it both ways. The unborn is either a life or it isn't; society can either establish criteria to terminate that life or it can't. Those on the extremes force us to analyze our theological beliefs. Once we decide what our core beliefs are, our decisions on those issues are already made, even if we disagree on the criteria. Without their constant haranguing, we could easily slip important issues under the rug, and avoid having to make the tough decisions of what it is we really believe.

I also really appreciate the passion of those on the periphery. They are true believers. I wish those who preach love, compassion, and accommodation had as much passion as those who preach judgment, division, and exclusion. Maybe we shouldn't elect a president who is an extremist, but we do need to listen to them. Hopefully some of their passion will rub off on us all.

APPENDIX C-4

This article first appeared in the
Wesleyan Christian Advocate
June 27, 1997

Death vs. Compassion

By Jim Nelson

The Timothy McVeigh trial generated a lot of discussion about the death penalty. McVeigh does indeed make it difficult to support abolition of the death penalty. He did coldly and calculatingly kill 168 people. His only defense was the incident in Waco. But what did his victims have to do with Waco? There is no excuse for his actions. No reasonable person could conclude there was any justification for what he did.

However, I still support the United Methodist Church's position against the death penalty. If McVeigh were given life in prison, I don't think he would be released any sooner than Charles Manson or Sirhan Sirhan. Prison is not the country club life some death penalty advocates want us to believe it is. Anyone who feels prisons are too easy should be forced to spend a week in one. They would change their minds.

But other cases make the implementation of the death penalty more difficult to defend, even though the crimes were equally heinous.

Take, for example, the case of Jesse Timmendequas, the man convicted of raping and killing Megan Kanka, the little girl "Megan's Law" is named after. Reportedly, he was beaten and sexually abused by his father and beaten and neglected by his mother. If behavior is learned, what behavior was he taught growing up? He may know what he did was wrong, but does he know how to do what is right?

In no way am I implying he should be excused for what he did. Timmendequas should never again be allowed to live in free society. He is and will remain a dangerous person. But does executing him solve the problem? Does it stop others who are growing up beaten and abused from raping and killing children in the future? Probably not. Timmendequas is not the only guilty party; he was the weapon someone else loaded and fired. Why are we not executing the person or persons guilty of creating Jesse Timmendequas?

Where were the courts and prosecutors when he was 10 years old and being abused by his parents? Where was the justice system when little Jesse Timmendequas was crying out for justice? Little boys are abused, then years later we are calling them monsters when they behave in the only way they were taught.

We must heal them as children to protect our own children. If a young boy in your neighborhood can't look you in the eye, walks with his head down and recoils when you reach out to touch him, meet his parents, be nosy, get involved in his life. Let him know how adults should behave. You might just help prevent a future tragedy.

Death is not the answer. Love, compassion, involvement in the lives of others is. Suffer the little children to come unto us.

APPENDIX C-5

This article first appeared in
The Georgia Guardian
June 4-10, 1999

Something To Die For

By Jim Nelson

Any cause worth killing for, ought to be worth dying for. For the last ten weeks, the United States, along with other members of NATO, has been bombing Kosovo and Yugoslavia. Our expressed justification for this action is humanitarian: protecting the thousands of ethnic Albanians who live in Kosovo. To do this, we are bombing their enemies; and if in the process, a few Albanians get killed – well; those are the costs of war.

We also don't seem to mind if a few innocent Serbian men, women and children get blown apart in the process. After all, those children should not have allowed the army to deport the Albanians and rape their women. If a few Chinese die when an errant NATO bomb lands on their embassy, that is OK too. Besides, haven't they been spying on us anyway?

But, when three US servicemen are captured, we go ballistic. We cry foul, and demand they be returned immediately. I hate to think what would happen if any U.S. soldier actually dies. There would probably be calls to nuke the entire country; to ethnically cleanse the Serbs from the face of the earth.

If this is really a humanitarian effort, if we are fighting the modern day equivalent of a Holy War, then why are we afraid to die for it? We seemed to have little problem putting our armed forces in harms way when the supply of cheap oil was threatened by the Iraqi invasion of Kuwait; thereby, threatening our standard of living.

The reality is that during these last two and a half months most of the ethnic Albanians have been removed from Kosovo. What have we accomplished?

During that time it appears hundreds, if not thousands, of Albanian men were brutally killed. Albanian women and young girls gang raped by soldiers and Albanians of all ages terrorized. What have we really done to stop any of these atrocities?

Sure, we indicted Slobadon Milosevic as a war criminal. Big deal. Does anybody actually believe he will ever stand trial? Of course, we have done everything we could to destroy the Yugoslavian economy and disrupt the lives of their citizens. But all we have really accomplished is the creation of a growing refugee crisis for neighboring Balkan countries.

If we truly believe the situation warrants military action, we need to act decisively. If we really care about the ethnic Albanians and what is happening to them, we need to be committed and willing to die for what we believe is right. If we are going to be the police of the world ensuring peace and tranquility around the globe, we need to be willing to put our lives on the line. If not, we should just shut up and stay out of other nations affairs.

Believe me, I am not a proponent of war. Even while serving as an airborne infantry office during the Vietnam war, I said there are several causes I am willing to die for, but very few I am willing to kill for; and I would never kill for anything I wouldn't die for. I just wish our national leaders, and those of the other NATO nations felt the same way.

APPENDIX C-6

This article first appeared in
The Georgia Guardian
June 19-25, 1998

State-Sponsored Prayer Erodes Religious Freedom

By Jim Nelson

Divine and/or Supreme Being or beings who may or may not exist, and who may or may not have created the universe, we pray, or perhaps we just say that we are grateful for this day, and for our school. We hope that we will be able to learn today, that we will respect the property of the school, that we will be kind to our teacher and to one another, and that we will not resort to violence. The end.

If a group advocating a constitutional amendment to allow school prayer gets its way, the above prayer, or one like it, might be approved. The courts will insist on such an innocuous prayer, aimed at offending no one and including everyone. Still, I would be willing to bet the first day it is used, someone will file suit in a federal court to have some or all of it changed. The only prayer that will ever be approved will be so watered down, most people will ask, "What's the point?" The problem is that in their attempts to offend no one, they will offend everyone.

Writing a prayer that will be acceptable to Christians, Jews, Muslims, Hindus, Buddhists, a well as Mormons, Branch Davidians, Heaven's Gaters and, of course, atheists will be impossible. A nation built on the concept of religious freedom cannot suddenly change and force a particular belief on school children. Trying to pass such a law will only point out religious intolerance, and in the end do more harm than good. Adults will engage in heated debates about what their children can and cannot be exposed to by others, creating even bigger divisions than those which already exist. The worst of each faith will be highlighted in the media and our children will be the big losers.

Freedom is something we lose one incremental step at a time. Developing a state-sanctioned prayer is an erosion of our religious freedom. We need to be careful about what we are asking for. We may just get it. The whole purpose of the First Amendment was to keep the state out of religion. We don't need to bring them into it now. Besides, if you are (insert your denomination here) and your child's teacher is (insert a faith you disagree with here), do you really want him or her giving your child religious instruction?

This is one time I agree with the president. Children can already pray in school. They can say the prayers of their particular faith before school, they can attend prayer groups, they can say grace before eating, they can even pray before taking a test. Parents can pray with their children before sending them off to school. They can pray at bus stops with other families, or in car pools on the way to school. Do we really need additional government intervention in our lives?

We need to stop looking to the government to raise our children for us, and stop abdicating our rights and responsibilities. If you want your children to pray, teach them yourself and set a good example by praying with them.

APPENDIX C-7

This article first appeared in
The Georgia Guardian
August 20-26, 1999

Keep Government Out of Religion

By Jim Nelson

In keeping with the adage, "Be careful what you pray for, you may get it," the Georgia Board of Education voted last week on the list of courses approved for our public schools. Included in the list were Bible I and Bible II, which it wisely referred to its attorneys for review. Although, these may sound like good moral courses for our young people to be taking, our public schools are not the best places to teach religion.

According to Linda Schrenko, state school superintendent, these are not religion classes. She says that the schools are merely going to teach the Bible as history with no mention of God, or creation. Plus, she says there is to be no interpretation as to what is true and what is myth.

Come on Linda, that is an impossibility. You cannot teach anything about the Bible without referring to God. After all, the whole Bible is about our relationship as humans with the Divine. How does the teacher answer the student who asks, did this really happen this way, or is this just a story someone made up to tell us about God and our relationship to God? Does that teacher say, "I'm not allowed to answer that question"? Do teachers present the ancient Israelites as being the chosen people of some unknown entity who helped them defeat their enemies, or as a fierce tribe who defeated larger armies all by themselves? How do they explain the birth stories of Jesus without referencing God, or any letters of Paul? I just cannot conceive of talking about the Bible without a specific theology being presented.

Who are these teachers going to be anyway? Are they going to be Biblical scholars who are fluent in Biblical Greek and Hebrew, and who have studied the history of the Bible in depth? Or, are they just going to be someone who took a Bible class in college? How can we be certain what they are teaching is consistent with current scholarship and not based on the Biblical theology of one denomination or another? And what translation of the Bible are they going to use? The King James, the New International, the New Revised Standard, the New Jerusalem, or some version edited specifically for the class? And, who does the editing?

Why is it people are always wanting the government, via the schools, to do what they are unwilling to do themselves? If people want the Bible taught to young people, their churches should develop Bible study classes for youths. If they want their version of the Bible taught, they should volunteer to teach it. We have to quit crying about the lack of morality in our schools and start teaching it ourselves in our own churches, our own neighborhoods, and our own homes. We cannot expect the government to fix everything.

Instead of teaching the Bible in the public schools, maybe our churches need to be asking why young people are not attending. Ask yourself, why is it supposedly good church members are so interested in having the schools do the church's job for them? Let the schools concentrate on teaching reading, writing and arithmetic, and let Sunday Schools teach the Bible.

APPENDIX C-8

The article first appeared in
The Georgia Guardian
September 18, 1999

FUNDING FAITH-BASED AFTER-SCHOOL PROGRAMS

By Jim Nelson

Last month several members of the state board of education wanted to post copies of the Ten Commandments in classrooms and teach Bible classes in the public schools. Now, other members of the board do not want churches to have after-school programs. At least not programs that receive any government funding. Georgia Attorney General Thurbert Baker recently issued an opinion questioning the legality of state grants that wind up going to religious organizations. The state board of education is asking him to look into their funding practices as well. On the surface, these positions seem to be at odds with one another, but in reality, they share a common trait: They are both wrong.

Last month, I wrote that religious education needs to take place in religious institutions and not be left up to the schools. Schools are not equipped to teach about God. However, churches are equipped to teach reading, writing and arithmetic. Many churches have classrooms that are empty all week. Holding after-school tutoring in those classrooms is an effective use of the space. Churches also have members willing to volunteer because they perceive helping children get a good start in life is an important ministry. This is one area where I agree with the Republican Party presidential front-runner, George W. Bush. He contends that many faith-based programs are effective and should qualify for federal funding.

The public schools are not staffed to handle the number of students who need special attention and assistance in learning the basics. Volunteers, and paid staff in churches are capable of doing just that. They can give the one-on-one attention many of these young children need to give them a competitive chance in the world.

As a nation, we have to get over our unreasonable fear of religion. Let's be realistic, everyone has a belief in structure and a theology. Those beliefs and their accompanying core values come through in what we do, and say. Whether someone is Jewish, Christian, Moslem, Buddhist, Atheist, secular humanist or some other religion, their beliefs are ultimately expressed in what they teach. Some of their beliefs are transmitted overtly and some subtly, but all of them are conveyed. When a program is offered in schools, parents do not know what beliefs are being taught to their children. However, when they send their children to a church, they expect some religious content even if it is only the images displayed in and around the room.

Government funding should be based on the effectiveness of the program, not on whether it is held in a religious setting or not. The questions asked should be, Does the performance of the students involved improve? If so, the program should be funded. If parents object to the religious content, they should take their children to another location. However, if we do away with faith-based programs, will there be enough quality programs to take their place or will students just be left out?

We have to start being reasonable. Too often we only look at the surface and fail to look deeper into the consequences of a program. Our goal should be to use government funds in the most effective manner possible, and not worry about whether anyone promises never to mention God. Besides, what is wrong with teaching children a little morality?

BIBLIOGRAPHY

Bartlett, John. *Familiar Quotations*, Sixteenth Edition, Justin Kaplan, General Editor. Boston: Little, Brown and Company, 1992.

Bercot, D. W. *Will the Real Heretics Please Stand Up*. Tyler, Texas: Scroll Publishing, 1989. As cited on the "Religious Tolerance" Web Site. URL: http://www.religioustolerance.org/execute.htm.

Birch, Bruce C. "The First and Second Books of Samuel" in *The New Interpreter's Bible: A Commentary in Twelve Volumes*, Leander E. Keck, ed. Nashville: Abingdon Press, 1998.

Bonhoeffer, Dietrich. *Letters and Papers from Prison,* Translated by Reginald H. Fuller. Macmillan Company, New York, 1953.

Carter, Stephen L. *The Culture of Disbelief*. New York: Basic Books, 1993.

Carter, Stephen L. *God's Name in Vain*. New York: Basic Book, 2000.

Constitution of the United States, The.

Fiorenza, Most Rev. Joseph A. A presentation to the 1999 U.S. Catholic Conference which was quoted on the "Religious Tolerance" Web Site.

URL: http://www.religioustolerance.org/execute.htm.

Fischer, Louis. *The Life of Mahatma Gandhi*. New York: Harper & Row Publishers, 1950.

Floyd-Thomas, Drs. Stacey and J. M. "Religion in American Life." And Internet class for Virginia Tech University. URL: http://smft.cis.vt.edu/rel2124.

"Four Christian Views of War." The Ministry Division of the General Assembly Council of the Presbyterian Church (U.S.A.). URL: http://www.horeb.pcusa.org/kosovo/four.htm.

Haynes, Jeff. *Religion in Global Politics*. London: Addison Wesley Longman Limited, 1998.

Holloway, Richard. *Godless Morality: Keeping Religion Out of Ethics*. Edinburgh: Canongate Books, Ltd., 1999.

Holy Bible, The, New Revised Standard Version. Division of Christian Education of the National Council of Churches of Christ in the U.S.A., 1989.

"Human Genome Project Information." From the United States Government Web Site. URL: http://www.ornl.gov/hgmis/elsi/behavior.html.

Lakoff, George. *Moral Politics: What Conservatives Know that Liberals Don't*. Chicago: The University of Chicago Press, 1996.

Kalas, J. Ellsworth. *Christian Believer: Knowing God with Heart and Mind – Study Manual*. Nashville: Abingdon Press, 1999.

Malcom X. A Spike Lee film. Burbank, CA.: Warner Brothers Production. 1992.

Marty, Martin E., with Jonathan Moore. *Politics, Religion, and the Common Good.* San Francisco: Jossey-Bass Publishers, 2000.

"Nature or Nurture." Article on the BBC News Web Site. URL: http://news.bbc.co.uk/hi/english/sci/tech/newsid_1164000/1164792.stm.

Nelson, Rev. James A. A weekly opinion column appearing in *The Georgia Guardian*. 1995-2000.

Nelson, Rev. James A. A bimonthly column entitled, "Faith and Politics" appearing in the *Wesleyan Christian Advocate*. 1996-present.

Prejean, Sister Helen, C.S.J. Quoted on the "Religious Tolerance" Web Site. URL: http://www.religioustolerance.org/execute.htm.

Seligman, Martin E. P., Ph.D. *What You Can Change & What You Can't: The Complete Guild to Successful Self-Improvement*. New York: Alfred A. Knopf, 1994.

Strong, Barrett, and Norman Whitfield. *War*, a song sung by Bruce Springsteen.

Swift, Jonathan. *Gulliver's Travels*. Garden City, N.Y.: Doubleday & Company, Inc., 1945.

Thoreau, Henry David. *Walden and Other Writings.* Joseph Wood Krutch, ed. Toronto: Bantam Books, 1962.

United Methodist Hymnal, The. Nashville: The United Methodist Publishing House. 1989.

Yoder, John Howard. *When War Is Unjust: Being Honest in Just-War Thinking*. Minneapolis: Augsburg Publishing House, 1984.

Printed in the United States
21873LVS00002B/58-60

9 781592 990832